I0605617

"This book is a gift. It teaches us not only to appreciate Ordinary Time in the church calendar but, more importantly, to be on the lookout for God in those many ordinary moments in life."

Andrew T. Abernethy, professor of Old Testament at Wheaton College and author of *Savoring Scripture*

"This book repeatedly brought me into contact with the holy and renewed my sense of the pervasive and persistent attention of God even, maybe even especially, in these segments of time where 'nothing' happens. Through her distinctively personal, reverent, and joy-filled voice, Amy Peeler blends story, readings of biblical narratives, and reflections on the church's liturgy in order to provoke an encounter between the reader and God. This is a book that will bring you to your knees in worship."

Aubrey E. Buster, associate professor of Old Testament at Wheaton College and author of *Remembering the Story of Israel*

"With theological depth and pastoral warmth, Amy Peeler invites readers into a deeper understanding of the longest and, perhaps, most underappreciated season of the church year. Ordinary Time is far from spiritually idle—it is where God does the daily, steady work of transformation. Peeler's reflections, rooted in Scripture, prayer, and the rhythms of the liturgical calendar, unveil the distinct beauty of this green and growing season. This book will speak to clergy and lay readers alike, whether they come from liturgical traditions or not. It is a welcome companion for the slow work of grace."

Porter C. Taylor, rector of the Church of the Good Shepherd and editor of *We Give Our Thanks Unto Thee*

"In a rich blending of memoir, liturgical commentary, and biblical meditation, this book invites us all to consider the long season of Ordinary Time an opportunity for deepening our spiritual roots. I am grateful for the connection points Amy Peeler highlights between moments in this season and their corresponding moments in Scripture. These points of convergence usher us along a journey with the church through key themes of faith. Should we follow Peeler's guidance on this journey, we will surely bear the spiritual fruit of discipleship."

James M. Arcadi, rector of All Souls Anglican Church and author of *An Incarnational Model of the Eucharist and Holiness: Divine and Human*

Amy Peeler
Esau McCaulley, SERIES EDITOR

Ordinary Time

The Season of Growth

Fullness of Time series

An imprint of InterVarsity Press
Downers Grove, Illinois

InterVarsity Press
P.O. Box 1400 | Downers Grove, IL 60515-1426
ivpress.com | email@ivpress.com

InterVarsity Press® is the publishing division of InterVarsity Christian Fellowship/USA®. For more information, visit intervarsity.org.

Cover design: Faceout Studio, Elisha Zepeda
Interior design: Daniel van Loon
Cover image: Butterfly caterpillar vintage art, Karen Arnold via publicdomainart.net

ISBN 978-1-5140-0968-0 (print) | ISBN 978-1-5140-0969-7 (digital)

Printed in the United States of America ♾

Library of Congress Cataloging-in-Publication Data
Names: Peeler, Amy L. B. author
Title: Ordinary time : the season of growth / Amy Peeler.
Description: Downers Grove, IL : IVP Formatio, [2026] | Series: Fullness of time series | Includes bibliographical references.
Identifiers: LCCN 2025031502 (print) | LCCN 2025031503 (ebook) | ISBN 9781514009680 hardcover | ISBN 9781514009697 ebook
Subjects: LCSH: Church year
Classification: LCC BV30 .P44 2026 (print) | LCC BV30 (ebook)
LC record available at https://lccn.loc.gov/2025031502
LC ebook record available at https://lccn.loc.gov/2025031503

31 30 29 28 27 26 | 13 12 11 10 9 8 7 6 5 4 3 2 1

To Lance,

who has shared my extraordinary days, ordinary days, and everything in between. I'm so grateful we've grown up together, and I look forward to spending the rest of our lives growing into the good God has for us.

Contents

The Fullness of Time

Series Preface

Esau McCaulley, Series Editor

Christians of all traditions are finding a renewed appreciation for the church year. This is evident in the increased number of churches that mark the seasons in their preaching and teaching. It's evident in the families and small groups looking for ways to recover ancient practices of the Christian faith. This is all very good. To assist in this renewal, we thought Christians might find it beneficial to have an accessible guide to the church year, one that's more than a devotional but less than an academic tome.

The Fullness of Time project aims to do just that. We have put together a series of short books on the seasons and key events of the church year, including Advent,

Christmas, Epiphany, Lent, Easter, and Pentecost. These books are reflections on the moods, themes, rituals, prayers, and Scriptures that mark each season.

These are not, strictly speaking, devotionals. They are theological and spiritual reflections that seek to provide spiritual formation by helping the reader live fully into the practices of each season. We want readers to understand how the church is forming them in the likeness of Christ through the church calendar.

These books are written from the perspective of those who have lived through the seasons many times, and we'll use personal stories and experiences to explain different aspects of the season that are meaningful to us. In what follows, do not look for comments from historians pointing out minutiae. Instead, look for fellow believers and evangelists using the tool of the church year to preach the gospel and point Christians toward discipleship and spiritual formation. We pray that these books will be useful to individuals, families, and churches seeking a deeper walk with Jesus.

Introduction

The Ordinary Season

When I traveled to the Holy Land for the first time, right before beginning this book, I was struck by how long it took to travel from one place to another. If that was true in a vehicle, how much more so would that have been true for Jesus on foot? Although I had recognized this intellectually for most of my life,[1] there in Israel I suddenly realized it in an embodied way. Jesus' life would have included many ordinary days, days in which he was simply walking from one place to another. His human experience was no less redemptive on those days than on the ones that he did or said something the inspired evangelists chose to record. In fact, for his work on those memorable days to be fully redemptive, it had to be interspersed with these ordinary days, because such is the experience of being truly and fully human. If Mary asked him at the end of many days of his life, as I might ask my own children, "What did you do today?" Jesus' answer, true for all intents and purposes, would be the same as theirs: "Nothing."

This is so often how the Lord works. God does a radical thing and then grants us time to reflect on it. If every day were radical, we could not take it in. Conversely, if there were no radical events that disrupted the world as we know it, it would be difficult to remember that God is always at work. Hence, the Lord gives us just the right balance between the extraordinary and the ordinary. The liturgical year aids believers' perception of this grace. It is during the ordinary times that we are given space for reflection, and through it, space to grow. We probably do most of our growing not in the midst of the radical but in reflection on it.

The many weeks of this season of the year are named as "ordinary" simply because they are arranged in an ordinal way—the weeks are counted one after another. When looking at a chart of the church year, you would notice that two different sections of Ordinary Time occur in the church calendar. The first takes place between Epiphany and Ash Wednesday, the second between Pentecost and Advent. The second and much longer season of Ordinary Time (as many as twenty-nine weeks) begins just as Eastertide ends. This second period of Ordinary Time continues until the liturgical year begins again with Advent, the "New Year" for the church.

It is also true that "ordinary" evokes the sense of "normal," and this is an apt description of these many weeks as well. It is neither a feast nor a fast season (although it includes many individual feasts). In other words, it is neither wholly celebrative nor dominantly mournful, but a largely repetitive season of ordinary weeks, one after another for dozens of them. Strikingly, that means that in the church, over half of the year is "ordinary."

Whether in the Northern or Southern Hemisphere, significant portions of these two ordinary seasons overlap with the long days of both winter and summer, the months in which schedules are often less hectic and, therefore, a period in which time seems to move a bit slower. But then a transition happens within the ordinary season, for it also includes the pivot to the new schedules of the school year, which, after a week or so of freshness, quickly settle into a routine. In different ways, the various time periods of this season include large swaths of repetitiveness. Only at the end of this liturgical season is something on the horizon that is truly not ordinary, the anticipation of Advent. Before then, and for a very long time, things are "normal." The seasons of the church year that are deemed "ordinary time" provide the appropriate setting to contemplate God's momentous and mundane works.

Prior to this project, I must admit that I dreaded Ordinary Time. Fed by excitement and change, this season seemed to offer little of either. It was simply something to get through until I could start preparing for Christmas. Writing this volume invited me to think differently about this season. The process of the project has opened my eyes not only to the necessity of the normal, but also to its distinct beauty. I have now been trained to see the blessed opportunities for growth in the gift of every normal day. I have learned that this season is not without the excitement of change, but that it is of a different kind, a slow but enduring kind of transformation. That kind of transformation is deeply, if not dramatically, exciting.

Other saints have helped me along the way. I have learned a great deal about these ordinary days from the powerful book by Tish Harrison Warren, *Liturgy of the*

Ordinary, which traces the presence of God from waking to sleeping and all the mundane moments in between.[2] In addition, *To Light Their Way* by Kayla Craig has served as a prayer guide for my family before I took up the writing of this book.[3] Craig trained me not to worry or gloat but to *pray* for all events in our lives, including the mundane ones. Finally, in the acclaimed Every Moment Holy series, long one of my favorites, I gained a foundational insight from Andrew Peterson, who riffs on Wendell Berry to remind readers that "there are only sacred moments and moments we have forgotten are sacred."[4] Even ordinary days and ordinary seasons cannot be boring when we have the eyes to notice God's presence and blessing with us in all things, patiently working with and in us to transform us more fully into the mature believers God intended us to be.

Ordinary Time among the people of God holds these two truths together, sacredness and simplicity. By virtue of creation, revelation, incarnation, and spiration God has elected to be present within the ordinary day-to-day of created life. We will not always be able to understand precisely how, but we can acknowledge that God is there in all things: the highs, the lows, and the in between; the radical as well as the common. As we are trained by the rhythms of the church year, we can more clearly know that God is with us and desires to grow us, even on the days when we are simply walking from one place to another.

Ordinary Prayers

A creative colleague and fellow church member has used her skills of artistry in graphic design to create a series of prayer cards. Printed on stately and solid paper with clean lines and elegant font, they display the prayers for each Sunday and major feast days of the church year. The colors of the liturgical year frame the prayer as well as fill in the Jerusalem cross at the top of each card.[5] She gifted our family with a set, and we've kept them in our dining room, where our family sits for dinner. It has been a joy week by week to have a visual reminder of the prayer we all prayed together each Sunday. These prayers provide an excellent window into the dynamic of the season.

As a convert to liturgical worship, I have not ceased to be amazed by the beauty and wisdom of theses prayers, woven from the language of Scripture and formed into poetry for liturgical worship. The collects for this Ordinary Time are gems, bequeathing worshipers such phrases as "Make us have perpetual love and reverence for your holy Name" (Proper 7), "Almighty God . . . you know our necessities before we ask and our ignorance in asking" (Proper 11), "God, you are always more ready to hear than we to pray, and to give more than we either desire or deserve" (Proper 22), and "You never forsake those who make their boast of your mercy" (Proper 18). These eloquent turns of phrase help us to grow to be more artful communicators of God's goodness.

The former rector of my parish, a church that often welcomes those, like me, who did not grow up with liturgy, explained that these prayers are called "collects" because they do just that—collect together all our thoughts into a unified prayer that expresses the focal theme of the day. Unsurprisingly, the collects come in communal language. They give voice to desires for the whole people of God. The prayers that collect our individual voices ask that the Lord might "cleanse and defend your Church" (Proper 13).[6] They ask that the gathered people, who are "built upon the foundation of the apostles and the prophets, Jesus Christ himself being the chief cornerstone" (Proper 8), may all "joyfully serve you in confidence and serenity" (Proper 3) and "proclaim your truth with boldness, and minister your justice with compassion" (Proper 6), as they "persevere with steadfast faith in the confession of your Name" (Proper 24). The collects are a great reminder that the Lord has good plans for us as individuals, but those cannot come to fruition if we remain on our own. God desires for us to grow *as a group*.

In the medieval calendar, the weeks of the second and much longer Ordinary Time were organized into four sub-periods. The first focused on invitation to Christian living, including the necessity of suffering. The second reflected on the righteous life that marks those who have received the grace of God. It begins with affirmations of who we are in Christ, through no merit of our own. We are invited to take hold of what is already true of us because of the grace of being grafted into Christ. This assurance drives believers into a healthy demonstration of faithfulness. Hence, the third section highlights the appropriate reaction to that grace, including works, very often manifest as acts of service to others. The final weeks begin moving the church to the contemplation of Advent as they focus on the rewards of righteous living. While some reshuffling has diffused this tightly organized system, these themes are still apparent throughout.[7] Suffering, grace, faithfulness, and the reward of God's abundance surface with most clarity in the prayers of the season.

As the church recognized that normal Christian living involves suffering, it is striking how often these collects ask for God's protection. Proper 13 is a prayer for God's defense of the church that states, "because [the church] cannot continue in safety without your help, protect and govern it always by your goodness" (Proper 13). If the church is following after Jesus, and he was hated and persecuted (John 15:18), the church should not be surprised that the powers and principalities will rise against them as well. God is therefore fittingly addressed as "the protector of all who trust in you" (Proper 12). For example, in one of the earliest prayers of the season, congregants ask God to "keep us . . . from all things that may hurt us" (Proper 2). Again, just two weeks later the church entreats God to "put away from us . . . all hurtful things (Proper 4). The reality is that injuries come not only from the outside but also from the inside, when Christian siblings intentionally or unintentionally hurt one another. Given this painful and all-too-common reality, the prayers are meant not only for protection but also for awareness. They are a preview of the part of the service in which we all join in the act of confession, inviting an investigation of the heart to see if there are places of unnamed hurt, received or given, even within the church.

Prayers that name the reality of suffering allow movement away from fear. Apprehension can keep one frozen, but by asking God for protection from any and all dangers and hurt, the church is freed to move into action. Growing things need to move, so it makes sense that in the season of growth, the church is praying for God's aid in its activity. The prayer for Proper 2 asks that the church, now reminded of God's protection, "may accomplish with free hearts those things which belong to your purpose."

A vocalization of the desire that faith be expressed in action is one of the most frequent themes in the collects of this season. Believers first need the inspiration of the Holy Spirit to think correctly so that then we can act correctly. This acknowledgment of the interdependent nature of our internal and external lives (Proper 5, 10, 14) appears, for example, in Proper 9, where the members of the church pray, "O God, you have taught us to keep all your commandments by loving you and our neighbor." The words the church says together articulate the basic and perpetually necessary call to be wholly devoted to

God in heart and action, echoing Israel's *Shema* (Deuteronomy 6:4) and Jesus' instruction to love God and love neighbor (Mark 12:30-31).

The weekly prayers of the season cause us to reflect together on the hardship of Christian life and God's provision in the midst of that hardship. When we say them together in worship, we hear our own voices join with the chorus of the voices around us, soft and loud, halting and confident, young and old. As a member of that group we are inspired to carry the chorus beyond the walls of the church, continuing to participate in the joy of fellowship and service. When the words of the prayers resonate in our minds and our lives throughout the week, we experience the ongoing growth of the abundant kingdom that is surely on its way.

The Season of Life and Death

I received the Every Moment Holy series as the last birthday gift my mother-in-law purchased for me before her death. I had heard friends rave about these books and therefore dropped a hint to her that this would be a lovely gift not only for me but also for our whole family. That she honored that desire by gifting me with a book of prayers we can use on a regular basis has left a powerful witness of her own strong intercession on our behalf. Now absent from the body and present with the Lord (2 Corinthians 5:8), I see no reason why her prayers do not continue for us who are still tethered to the daily patterns of time.

That pertinent juxtaposition of ongoing life in the shadow of death exposes one of the most ordinary of human realities. From the moment we are conceived, we are moving toward our own end. Between these two shoals of the ultimate, birth and death, we live out our days. And yet, as believers in Jesus, we do not do so as those without hope (1 Thessalonians 4:13). The bookends of our lives are encompassed into a grander story. Christians are blessed to know that human existence is not an endless repetitive cycle of days in the midst of a meaningless beginning and inevitable end; rather, human life has a purpose. God chose to create, and God chose to redeem, so that each human can know that all their days have the stamp of divine blessing.

As Douglas Kaine McKelvey notes in *Death, Grief, and Hope,* the second volume of the Every Moment Holy series, navigating between the shoals of birth and death is also true of our spirit's revived life with God. We are invited to actively participate in what God has accomplished for us in Jesus Christ. "From the moment of our baptism into the death of Jesus, we begin the practice of dying by degrees—dying to self and to our self-centered pursuits of anything that wars against our vocation as disciples."[8] It is a grief that our bodies disintegrate toward death (faster for some than others, though it is inevitable for all). Conversely, it is a joy that our spirits can mature throughout our time on earth. They are also, by degrees, dying to the disease of sin that impacts us. Ordinary Time affords us the space to contemplate the normality, by nature, of our bodies' groaning for redemption and also the *new* normality, by grace, of our spirit's becoming more like Christ. In the state of the world in which we live, physical growth and strength last but a season, but spiritual growth, which begins at our rebirth in Christ, will continue.[9] As we learn to allow growth in the here and now, we will perpetually practice those skills of growing as we continue to mature into God's inexhaustible glory forever. What we learn and practice during Ordinary Time, this season of growth, is preparation for eternity.

Our entire lives have now been sacralized by the growing eternal life we have because of the life, death, and resurrection of the Son of God, Jesus the Messiah. The readings of this season reflect our connection to Christ. The Gospel readings during the first period of Ordinary Time (as many as nine weeks) focus on early events in the life and teaching of Jesus, including his mission to the Gentiles, a natural outflow of the visit of the Magi. The readings begin with recalling his baptism and culminate in his transfiguration, celebrated right before Lent begins. The second period of Ordinary Time (twenty-nine weeks) begins with the remembrance of Jesus' departure (Easter/Ascension/Pentecost) and concludes before we anticipate his arrival (Advent). The readings remind us that it is his life that now counts our days. Now that Jesus has come, "ordinary" is what it has never been before. Hemmed in by our own birth and death, by virtue of our confession in Christ, our days now unfold within the reality of his birth, death, and resurrection.

I trace the unfolding of our lives in his life through the seven chapters of this book. The first four focus on key motifs that pervade the entire season, the season's color of green that signifies growth, the season's remembrance of bold faith, the season's initial celebration and then continual praise of our triune God, then finally, the season's (and really, *every* season's!) foundational participation in the Lord's Supper. The next three chapters explore some of the biblical readings from this time of the church year, those texts that tell the stories of the family with whom God makes covenant. This family, through both normal life and extraordinary events, teaches us to have faith in God. They see God and trust God. Contemplating their stories moves us to show gratitude to God for the redemptive work previewed in the life of this family and then fully realized in Christ. My hope is that reflection on these themes and texts may open your eyes, as mine have been, to the mighty wonder of this normal, common, mundane-but-never-boring, Christ-shaped ordinary season.

1

Green

For the past several years, I've been on a mission to find green shoes. Priests have few opportunities for self-expression in our uniform liturgical dress. Shoes and earrings are really my only options for creativity. Because this season is the longest of all, I've accrued quite a few green earrings, but until recently the shoes had eluded me. That is, until I discovered a great treasure in my local thrift store: a decent pair of green tennis shoes, in a brand that even my high school daughter considered cool. The light green of the shoes complements the vibrant green of my stole and chasuble, and the style conveys the casual coolness of summer. I like them so much that I am truly excited to wear them for multiple weeks of the year.

The color green—the color of this ordinary season—visually reminds participants of growth, of fresh buds and lush grass. It signifies life and growth corresponding to the weeks we read about the life of Jesus, the growth of the church, and the discipling work of the Holy Spirit. Depending on location, green might be the prominent hue outside as well, in the trees and in the fields. The connection with the greens of nature allows worshipers to consider the signs of growth and new life in their own hearts and congregations.

True Colors

I was intrigued to learn from my elementary school son a few years ago, thanks to his inspiring teacher, that leaves are not naturally green. Leaf colors come from pigments, and as we might remember from our own teachers, the green color in leaves comes from the pigment chlorophyll. Other pigments make leaves orange, yellow, or red, depending on the variety of the tree. Leaves always have pigments in them that manifest as other than green, but we cannot see these colors until the fall. Then, due to a change in temperature and a decrease in sunlight, leaves stop making chlorophyll. Although green is the color in which the leaves are born and the color they display for the majority of their lives, it is not their inherent hue. Instead, it is when the leaves begin to change in the fall, just as Ordinary Time is reaching its end in the Northern Hemisphere, that the leaves reveal their distinct individual colors. They were present all along but not visible. We might say that all summer they've clothed themselves in something that is not their own. The radiance of the sun creates chlorophyll, which overlays their underlying pigmentary identity. Only as the rays grow less direct and the temperature cools does the chemical process cease, and then we see the variety of what their colors are without the sun. As the leaves get closer to their own end, when they fall to the ground and decompose—their own death, as it were—we see their underlying color. Conversely, as they are closer to birth and more exposed to the sun, the source of life, we see them in green.

The life cycle of a leaf resonates with our life in Christ in several ways. In one of the best-known baptismal formulas in the New Testament, Paul tells the Galatians that they have been clothed with Christ (Galatians 3:27). This is fitting language for baptism because, at certain times in the church, baptism was conducted in the nude, an evocation of the rebirth it displays. After emerging from the water, the baptizand was wrapped in new clothes.[1] Having shed their former garments of slavery, they now wear the royal mantle of God's family (Galatians 4:7).

Consider how differently you navigate the world when you are in stained sweatpants as opposed to a tailored suit. When I'm dressed very casually in public spaces, often in clothes used to run or lift weights, I feel my body posture change; it becomes drawn in and apologetic for my grime. On the other hand, when dressed in professional and smart attire, I become straight backed and hold my head high, ready to do good work in the world. Clothing is not only about personal feelings but also can change the dynamics of interaction. Fairly or not, people often respond to us differently based on how we are dressed.

If these things are true for clothing that will fade away, how much more so is this the case for our permanent embrace by the living Lord. Even though Paul is using the imagery of clothing to communicate his point, that metaphor does not capture the full power of the change he describes. To be baptized into Christ is not only external but also exerts an internal change. Paul asserts that when we are baptized, we are filled with Christ's Spirit, the Holy Spirit. Because of this holistic reality, when we are clothed with Christ, we begin to live like him. In other words, this is not just about how we feel—it is an actual and supernaturally-rendered change. We grow in the fruit of the Spirit as our hearts and minds are renewed. The closer we are tethered to the reality of our baptism, the better we remember the presence of our new clothes, the more like Christ we stay. To be clothed with Christ should change how we think about ourselves. Not because we deserve it, but because of God's grace, we've been clothed with the honor of Christ. We can hold our heads high. To be clothed with Christ also affects how we receive one another. We meet each other as we would encounter Christ, and so utmost honor is due to those brothers and sisters who bear his name and don his royal garments.

In churches that utilize the liturgical colors during Ordinary Time, believers can consider the verdant green in the sanctuary as a visual reminder of this truth about their lives. They are clothed with the life of Jesus Christ in baptism. As they respond to the One who is the radiance of God (Hebrews 1:3) by the power of the Holy Spirit, they too will more frequently and more vibrantly and verdantly display his life, in how they consider themselves and in how they consider one another.

The foliage of deciduous trees silently yet vibrantly proclaims another truth about gospel life. Leaves do not cease to be the color that they are, but for the long period of spring and summer, they respond to the light of the sun and are clothed with green. So, too, we might say that members of the church are a beautiful variety of reds and yellows and oranges, different beautiful bodies and personalities and giftings. The congregants in Galatia did not cease to be Jews or Greeks, males or females, but they were enveloped by Christ as they would put on lavish robes. Our natural yellows and oranges and reds—or, in the language of Galatians 3:28, our maleness and femaleness, as well as our ethnicities—are not lost. They are still there, a vital part of who God created us to be, and because they are created by God, they are beautiful and good. Nevertheless, much like works, they are insufficient on their own to lead to life. If our natural selves are all we see, we are tipping toward death, not because it is bad to be Jew or Gentile, male or female, but because the world that God created good is currently marred by sin and stands in need of redemption. When, however, through faith, we are freed from sin and death, in Christ we become more fully who God created us to be. Our different hues are not eliminated but incorporated. We do not lose our particularity when we are baptized into Christ. Instead, we become more fully human as we grow into his image, who is the template for all humanity as *the* image of God (2 Corinthians 4:4; Colossians 1:15). As Irenaeus said, the glory of God is a human fully alive.[2]

When we put on Christ, we have a new ordinary, an ordinary in which we can be the men and women, Jews or Gentiles who grow into the blessings of God. We are rooted in the confidence of knowing our value as created in God's image and also rooted in the confidence of knowing our beauty as made new in Christ. It is also true that in Christ we are all clothed with his life, all clothed with green. Hence, in addition to our diversity, we all share a unity. We can expect our fellow Christ-confessors to treat us with the honor due to him as we offer the same respect to them as we join together in our various vibrancy, united in the verdant life of Christ.

True Freedom

In addition to a new life now, being baptized into Christ opens us to a new future to which we can look forward. As those baptized into Christ, we become the free children of God looking forward to the blessing of an eternal inheritance (Galatians 3:18, 29; 4:7).[3] Those familiar with the pairings in Galatians 3:28 may notice that

I left out one pair: the enslaved and the free. This is intentional. If Ordinary Time is the season of growth, it is the time in which the good of God's creation grows into greater maturity in Christ. In Christ, men become more fully the men they are meant to be, and women become more fully the women they are meant to be. The beautiful ethnicities and cultures that make up the nations who worship God are amplified in Christ.[4] Unlike these things that make a person who they are, namely, the God-given embodiment of sex and ethnicity, it is not the case that slaves become more fully slaves when they are baptized into Christ. Sex and ethnicity are blessed gifts of God. Slavery and ownership are not. There is no way to find more good in a system in which one human owns another, because there is no good in that system to begin with.

Readers might immediately counter that Christians become slaves to the God who willingly took the form of a slave (Philippians 2:5-11). This is true, but the distinction is radical. To willingly choose to be a slave to God, who is Creator and not part of creation, is entirely different from being enslaved to another human. Slavery has no part in God's creation, nor does it ever receive God's blessing.[5] Paul's letter to Philemon builds on the ideal of freedom in Israel's Scriptures to show that the New Covenant ideal in the church is also the obliteration of human slavery. There, Paul urges Christians to treat one another as siblings and not as property (Philemon 16).

In Galatians itself, Paul makes clear that the pair "slave and free" is different from the others. To clarify this point, Paul spends time talking about slavery both before and after verse 28. Hence, for those who are currently enslaved when they are baptized into Christ, their slave status is not amplified; rather, it is radically changed. In Christ, those who are slaves get the benefits of the free. Instead of a lifetime of slavery with nothing left to them at the end, no hope for a future, they instead get an inheritance from God. Slaves are freed. Slaves are adopted. Slaves become children. Slaves become heirs. Reflecting on this aspect of the true green of freedom in Christ provides a powerful connection to the holidays of freedom celebrated during Ordinary Time in America: Juneteenth and Independence Day. Freedom in Christ is a perfect and enduring liberty that the imperfect national freedom, for which we can be both grateful and also honest about its exclusions, can only ever serve as a shadow to a greater reality.

The difference in the way the slave/free pair works out in Paul's argument points to the freedom present in the other pairs as well. In Christ, any enslaving practice that arises out of our identity as we live it out in a sinful world is also obliterated in Christ. If aspects of our ethnicity or gender enslave us to our own sinful desires, or if they are used by others to enslave us to their limitations that run contrary to the freedom of God's kingdom, these aspects should not be a part of our new and true life in Christ. Racism and sexism enslave both the perpetrator and the victim. They have the hue of brimstone, not the vibrancy of life.[6]

Viewing this long season through this verdant lens reminds me to have patience and hope. Just as it takes time for plants to grow and change, God's work on a corrupted and willful creation takes a long time. It takes patience to yield as God molds us more fully into the image of Christ. God's steady work in this process also gives us hope. God will cause all things to grow into maturity.

When we see the green leaves and green grass outside the church and the green vestments and decorations inside, we are invited to cultivate our lives to be rooted more deeply in our baptism into Christ. Having been enveloped by him, our individual colors are still beautifully present, and over them we are surrounded by his abundant and eternal life. In those robes, we may walk with the confidence of freedom and the deference of honoring others as we would honor Christ himself. He is the source and aim of our life. This verdant season sets our new, true, and glorious ordinary existence before our eyes, as it grows week by week. It might not be a bad idea to clothe ourselves in green for this season, all the way down to our shoes.

2

Bold

Because this season is known as the "ordinary" one, we might expect it to be a long stretch with neither "feast-day nor fast."[1] On further reflection, it becomes clear that given our new, enduring, and abundant life in Christ, believers cannot help but celebrate. The period of time is marked out, in fact, by two Sunday festivals. At the beginning believers honor Trinity Sunday (for the West) or All Saints (for the East) and at the end, Christ the King.

I begin, however, with a different feast, that which commemorates Mary's visit to her kinswoman Elizabeth (Luke 1:36-56). Because it is a set feast and the seasons around it shift, depending on the date of Easter for that year, it might fall within Ordinary Time. Even more important, it marks some of the earliest moments in the incarnate life of our Lord, the life which makes ours possible. It is also fitting to contemplate during this season because the lessons of bold proclamation enable the church to carry on the same kind of bold testimony throughout this season of growth.

The church celebrates the Annunciation, the day that Gabriel invited Mary to offer her life to facilitate God's salvation of the world (Luke 1:26-38), on March 25, exactly nine months before the celebration of Jesus' birth on December 25. Our God often works surprisingly through the messiness of life, and so an immaculate Savior need not have gestated for nine months to the day. Nevertheless, the church's desire to honor the perfections of God is a respectable one. The pattern continues with the birth of John, celebrated on June 24. Since Luke notes that Elizabeth was six months pregnant at the time of the Annunciation (Luke 1:26), the forerunner's birth was imagined to have happened one day shy of perfection, on the twenty-fourth rather than the twenty-fifth. To be faithful to Luke's recounting, Mary's visit to Elizabeth needs to be honored between the Annunciation and the birth of John.

If the Gospel of Luke was the only guide, the date would fall earlier in that window of time. For, according to Luke, Mary left "with haste" after the Annunciation to visit Elizabeth "in those days" (Luke 1:39). The eighty miles between Nazareth and Ein Karem, the traditional village of Zechariah and Elizabeth, would have taken about a week to traverse. In addition to the fact that it is hilly terrain, most women experience some sickness or at least extreme tiredness at the beginning of a pregnancy. It is unlikely that Mary traveled alone, given her physical state and the culture at the time, so she might have had to wait to join others who were making the trip south. These factors may not have allowed her departure to be as hasty as if they were not present. Even so, Luke also notes that she stayed with Elizabeth "for about three months" (Luke 1:56) before the birth of John, who was already six months in utero when Jesus was conceived (Luke 1:26). Given these factors, if the Annunciation is celebrated on March 25 and John's birth on June 24, then sometime in early April seems a better time for the celebration of Mary's visit than the late-May date set by the church calendar.

Exegesis alone did not determine when to celebrate the Visitation, however. Various Christian groups had different days of honoring it, but it was set on May 31 by Pope Urban VI near the end of the fourteenth century.

This was the time of the Great Schism, when more than one pope was claiming legitimacy. Urban decreed that this day be set for the celebration in hopes that the Mother of God and her demonstration of deep relationship with a female family member very different from her—one who was older, long-barren, and from a different town—might facilitate the restoration of the unity of the church.

On my first visit to the traditional site of this meeting, I discovered that it is nestled in the midst of beautiful country. Not only is it breathtakingly mountainous but also the village of Ein Karem is now an artist colony, full of expressions of the loveliness of God-given human creativity. The village spring is at the bottom of the hill, surely where Mary and Elizabeth would have visited. Christians, however, have claimed that, because he was a priest, Zechariah lived at the top of a hill in a stately home—one that included its own spring. The climb up was not for the faint of heart, a testament to Mary's strength, especially in the state of early pregnancy.

At the top of the hill, pilgrims are greeted with a visual feast. With the picturesque view of the valley in the background, Mary's word of praise, *Magnificat,* is constructed out of rose-colored stone and frames the entrance to the site. The airy courtyard boasts a metal statue of Mary and Elizabeth, but even with this durable medium, the artist has captured the gentleness and joy on their faces. On the wall are dozens of "Magnificats" in more languages than were spoken at Pentecost, decorated with a variety of distinct but complementary floral patterns, a testament to the fact that Mary's words have become the prayer of the church among every beautiful tribe and tongue. The paintings of various scenes in Mary's life around and within the structures are vibrant, even though I had to acknowledge that the clothing would be more fitting in a Jane Austen film than the first-century Judean hill country. Although I've had the privilege of being exposed to a significant amount of Marian art, I found these interpretations unusual and fresh. The artist has captured the beauty of the terrain one has seen just outside, the agedness of Elizabeth, and the blessing of holiness bestowed on Mary.

The bottom level of the site preserves Elizabeth and Zechariah's house; on top of it sits a church. This is how humans treat holy space. When God has determined that something important happens in a particular location, believers retain that location. When more space or more beauty is needed to honor that event, they do not tear down what is there or build in another location; rather, they build on top of it, creating a mound of the holy all the way down. As I entered into that high-ceilinged resonate room, I had no trouble believing that if Christians had remembered this space, then it claimed a high likelihood of being the location where Mary greeted Elizabeth. I was persuaded by the possibility that it was in this very place where the elder woman was filled with the Holy Spirit, and, by that inspiration, proclaimed a blessing on Mary as the exemplar for all who trust in the perfect fulfillment of God's promises (Luke 1:45). It was easy for me to trust that here Mary uttered the Magnificat, her soul overflowing in praise to God. In the quietness of a whisper, I added my voice as I recounted her prayer, in my own native tongue, the English translation from the Book of Common Prayer (BCP). I so wished others could join me to chant it. Nevertheless, even my solo and barely audible attempt filled my heart with joy. There are times in life we simply cannot wipe the smile off our face. Our body displays the contents of our heart, and we cannot be silent. This was one of those occasions.

The church of our era, not unlike the Catholic Church of the late 1300s, also finds itself in a state of deep disunity.

The causes are many, but, interestingly, Mary stands at the center of several controversies. Christians have arrived at very different conclusions about what one should believe about her and how her life might point toward God's plan for Christians living today. How much respect toward her is appropriate? What does her life indicate for the lives of women in the church? What does the Magnificat, which proclaims God's right-side upping of the world, demand for our participation in God's justice today?

Throughout my trip to the Holy Land, including the visit to Ein Karem, I expected that God might show me that my passion for Mary's story might need to abate. I anticipated (as a good Anglican) that I might be shown ways that my zeal to share the good news about God's invitation to her should be tempered and come to a respectable moderation. Thankfully, faithful siblings have pointed out ways I can be more careful as I share the story of God's choice to involve her in the birth and ministry of Jesus. In the land of Israel, there were times that I was convicted of a lack of kindness in my zeal.

To my great surprise, however, time and time again, I was much more deeply and persistently convicted of the opposite. My love for the study and proclamation of God's grace and power through Mary's life was not wrong. I was convicted that instead of apologizing for it or choosing to be quiet about it, I, like Mary, should boldly and joyfully proclaim the goodness of the Lord revealed in an unparalleled way in her story. Her Magnificat uttered on that plot of land thousands of years ago is not an expression of Victorian femininity, genteel and passive "niceness." It is an unapologetic proclamation of the sovereignty and grace of God, who will topple the proud and the powerful and exalt the humble and meek (Luke 1:52-53).

Sometimes the cure for disunity is not compromise and silence, but boldness, an irrepressibly joyful proclamation that God values all people, often by showing a preference for those who are not typically valued. This is dangerous territory, of course, because scoundrels too think they are right. The hard of heart speak loudly and shun compromise. Hence it is vital that Mary did not utter this song alone. If she had been praising herself, airing her grievances, and preparing to fight the power with her own power, the older-and-wiser, Spirit-filled Elizabeth would have corrected her. Stepping into the vulnerable open space of bold praise to our radical God takes an immense amount of discernment, one's own and with one's community. Maybe that is why I could not bring myself to shout out the Magnificat in that sacred and fitting space, because, at that moment, I was on my own.

The Feast of the Visitation on May 31 falls at a time of transition into a new season for many. In the Northern Hemisphere, the weather is truly edging into warmth. For academics, terms are coming to an end before summer break. For Americans, this falls right after Memorial Day, the beginning of the season of summer. It is a fitting day to reflect on this event in the freshness of this season, to contemplate the joyful reunion of two women who give voice to the fact that God, through their faith, is graciously redeeming and setting the universe right. This inbreaking of divine beauty once proclaimed in and now preserved by this exquisitely beautiful space will not be welcomed by the powers and principalities who prefer the comfort of their own ugliness. So, the freshness of this transitional day invites celebrants to ask the Lord for a community of wisdom to determine where they need to humble themselves and admit their wrongs, and where they need to be uncompromisingly bold in magnifying the Lord, so that the church might achieve not a union of superficial and fake civility, but like the deep friendship between differently-situated Elizabeth and Mary, a true unity achievable only in the power of the Holy Spirit.

Timothy Dudley-Smith's modern hymn "Tell Out My Soul" sets the Magnificat into a fresh poem. He captures the verve and the tenderness of that moment as well as how it has comforted and empowered millennia of Christians. Our church often sings it during Ordinary Time, usually around August 15, in another feast that celebrates Mary in this season. Catholic and Orthodox believers celebrate her Assumption into heaven, or "Repose in the Lord," on this day, and Anglicans have revived it as another day to remember her. I believe it is a good moment to reflect on the endurability of her faith, through the life of Jesus as well as into the early era of the church (Acts 1:14). It is also good to acknowledge the endurability of her words, first shared with Elizabeth, captured in sacred Scripture by Luke, and utilized as the prayer of the church. In many traditions, Mary's Magnificat is the prayer spoken or sung at the daily evening service. It is such a gift to proclaim what is true about God. By exalting the humble and dismantling pride by the revelation of Jesus Christ, God is magnificent. I need that reminder at the beginning of Ordinary Time as well as multiple weeks into the season. Like those who compiled the portions of Evening Prayer must also have believed, I need that reminder every day of my life.

To remember and honor what happened between two women in a home two millennia ago can set the tone and strengthen the nerve of believers throughout this ordinary season. Yet again, it is the case that something ordinary, the ordinariness of women talking, transforms into something extraordinary *because they are talking about God's work in Jesus Christ.* God uses their encounter and the songs of praise sung therein to make every day that follows much more than ordinary. No matter our circumstances, it is true that "God, remembering his mercy, hath holpen his servant Israel; as he promised to our forefathers, Abraham and his seed for ever" (BCP). Hence, we can believe that, ultimately, all will be well. Because God provided that help through Mary in her son Jesus, we, as beneficiaries of the gift of the same Holy Spirit, are never without access to that same source of superordinary strength. Joining in with these women as they boldly praise God—in feast and fellowship, prayer and song—enables the church to grow. As we grow, we can continually and boldly say, "My soul doth magnify the Lord."

3

Triune

When I was ordained as a priest, it was in a group of two. I had the privilege of going through the process with another bi-vocational academic. For our ordination service, we each got to select a hymn. Hers was "I Bind Unto Myself Today," the great trinitarian hymn set to the tune "Saint Patrick's Breastplate," so named because this text has been connected to the Roman-become-slave Patricius. In the early 400s he met Christ and then returned to evangelize the country where he had been enslaved. The familiar English translation is the work of a godly Irish woman, Cecil Frances Alexander, wife of the bishop of Ireland in the mid-1800s.[1] The words of her translation recount the power of the strong name of the Trinity revealed in creation, in God's protection against evil, but chiefly in Christ. Our Lord Jesus is, the singer proclaims, "with me, within me, behind me, before me, and beside me" to do all that is necessary in every situation. Fittingly, for such a meaningful service, we sang all seven robust verses. While normally this kind of respect for hymns warms the heart of my church-organist husband, on that particular day, he was less than excited. That day had not only demanded travel and a great many details to be organized with three young children in tow, but he had also been struck by a stomach virus. When I passed him as I processed down the aisle, he was white as a sheet and holding on to the pew in front of him for dear life. On that day, that hymn seemed longer than eternity.

Trinity Sunday

Every time I sing this hymn on Trinity Sunday, the first Sunday after Pentecost, the first Sunday of Ordinary Time, I cannot help but recall that memory. When I sing it now outside of such a weighty and stressful moment, I am able to give more attention to these bold and beautiful words. Christ's power upholds and shields us in our weakness and in our victories. We are marked with the very name of God as Christ embraces us into his life, granting us knowledge of God's work in creation and a membership in God's long and faithful work with Israel and the church.

This powerful and ancient hymn ushers congregations into the contemplation of the triune God, who elected not to remain distant from the brokenness of humanity but to bind our condition to himself. The result of this intimacy, shockingly, is not that God's perfection is tarnished but that our weakness is steadily transformed into his likeness of majesty and strength.

The doctrine of the Trinity was not invented to assuage intellectual and theological boredom but was the only fitting response to what early believers experienced of God. We know Triunity to be true about God because God has revealed it to be so, in the person and work of the Son and the Spirit. As the epistle reading for this Sunday in Year A from 2 Corinthians 13 affirms, we know that God is triune because we've experienced grace from Jesus Christ, love from God the Father, and the fellowship of the Holy Spirit (2 Corinthians 13:14). Because believers today experience the same God, trinitarian language gives us the words we need to express what we know is true of God. We know that God the Father communicates through creation and through the prophets. We are aware that the Son revealed the Father. We experience the reality that the Spirit connects us to the life of

God now that Jesus has ascended to the right hand of the Father.

The Trinity is an incredibly complicated Christian doctrine. It cannot be ignored due to its difficulty, however, because it stands at the center of all other doctrines. The season of Ordinary Time begins with a celebration of this truth, but not in an effort to invite congregants to master it. Instead, we celebrate to remind ourselves that we cannot comprehend the being of God. Even within our limited understanding, however, we can still worship the One who is the ground of all being and life, including our own. Some church leaders resisted honoring the Trinity on a specific Sunday since the truth should be proclaimed weekly,[2] but I disagree. An intentional reminder of that which is always present is beneficial for humans, who may overlook what has become common by repetition. By taking a day to honor a truth about God that we name every week with every prayer, we intentionally affirm that the Trinity is not an esoteric theological puzzle but the source of the whole of our lives.

Knowing the triune God changes our lives, and that process of transformation is born out of proper worship. Proper worship begins when we confess the God being worshiped—namely, the God who is triune. The opening collect for this week captures the guardrails that hold the infinite depth of this doctrine. We pray both to "acknowledge the glory of the eternal Trinity" as well as "to worship the Unity." These words hold together the uncompromising affirmation that our God is three persons and that our God is One. Similarly, the proper preface for this day celebrates the "One and equal glory of you, O Father, and of the Son, and of the Holy Spirit."

The lectionary texts for the day either celebrate God as Creator by hearing the account of creation and praising God for it in Genesis 1:1–2:4 and Psalm 8, or they remember Isaiah's encounter with the holy God recounted in Isaiah 6. The New Testament readings feature several of the many passages that prompted the church to articulate this truth about God, passages where there is unmistakable unified divine action of the Father, the Son, and the Spirit.

As I proceed out of the church on Trinity Sunday, we often sing the great Reginald Heber (1783–1826) hymn "Holy, Holy, Holy." It captures the central claim of the day, "God in three Persons, blessed Trinity," in a rousing and inviting way. It gathers our voices with the heavenly praise of cherubim and seraphim who extol God as merciful and mighty. The song also recognizes where we might find ourselves on any given Sunday, weighed down by the blindness of our own eyes or the eyes of others, with a sense that darkness can hide God from us. Even and especially in those times, which for many are frequent enough that they might well be called "ordinary," we can proclaim that the God who we cannot see is "perfect in power, in love, and purity." Liturgical scholar Philip Pfatteicher fittingly reminds us, "The Church worships not the doctrine nor even the mystery, but God."[3] The Trinity is the beginning point of this season because confessing the Trinity is the beginning of the Christian life. This celebration has been so important that some churches refer to the subsequent weeks of the season as the "weeks after Trinity."

Trinity Season

While Trinity Sunday occurs only once each year, multiple elements of the liturgical worship service continue to remind congregants of their triune God each week. Ordinary Time repeatedly gives worshipers opportunity not only to learn about and mentally assent to, but also to *confess* the triunity of God. This confession most often takes place as the church joins together in prayer. From the beginning of the gathering until the end, congregants participate in prayers that point to the church's incorporation into the triune life of God.

Opening Collect. The opening collects throughout the season display a trinitarian shape. When congregants ask that God "graft in our hearts the love of your Name," then we are able to acknowledge that it is the triune God—Father, Son, and Holy Spirit—who initiates the fruit of good works in our lives (Proper 17). Only by God's triune power could we "continually be given to good works" (Proper 23) and love what God commands (Proper 25). We ask for these good things "of which we are not worthy to ask, except through the merits and mediation of Jesus Christ, our Savior" (Proper 22). He serves as the template for right living as we ask for grace to "receive thankfully the fruits of his redeeming work and to follow daily in the blessed steps of his most holy life" (Proper 15). We acknowledge to God that, on our own, "we are not able to please you," and so also acknowledge our dependence on the gift of the Holy Spirit who "may in all things direct and rule our hearts" (Proper 19). When we have the opportunity to pray such prayers corporately, they echo in our hearts as we leave the gathering, reminding us that the triune power of God goes with us all until we can gather again.

Eucharistic Prayer. The prayers of the Eucharist continue to invite us to participate in God's triune life. As the service moves from the Liturgy of the Word to the liturgy of the sacrament, the Eucharistic portion beings with a prayer fitting to the day or the season. Hence, it is called the "proper preface." Between the *sursum corda* (when the priest says, "Lift up your hearts") and the *sanctus* (when the priest and the congregation say, "Holy, holy, holy"), the person leading out in the celebration of the Lord's Supper voices a prayer of thanksgiving for an attribute or action of God. In the many ordinary Sundays of this season, these prayers, or proper prefaces, take a triune shape by focusing on the Father, the Son, and the Holy Spirit.

In the prayer to the Father, the congregation is led to praise God as the source. The early Christian James affirms that the Father of lights is the giver of all good things (James 1:17), so also this prayer praises God the Father who is "the source of light and life." By utilizing "light" language, the prayer affirms that God's divine life is fully radiant. This is a good reminder that, just as darkness is not an entity on its own but simply the absence of light, so too any evil we experience in our lives is a privation and not an independent power. Although those who come to steal, kill, and destroy God's people (John 10:10) wreak real havoc, they have no ultimate power that might someday defeat God. They act not out of strength but out of the weakness of not submitting to and drawing from God's goodness. Knowing that darkness cannot abide in the sphere of light, we can rest in the knowledge that God, as the source of light, will ultimately overcome any evil we experience.

In naming the Father as the source of life, the prayer assents to the divine order, or taxis, discerned by the Christian tradition as made evident in the Scriptures. The Father begets the Son and sends the Spirit, but since the Son and the Spirit are also eternal God, there is no chronology in this relationship. In other words, there is no time in which the Son and the Spirit were not. Light imagery aids our understanding of God's triune life. As a source of light immediately emits light, so is it the case that God the Father as the source of the Son and the Spirit is never without the Son or the Spirit. It is out of the abundance of the eternal triune life that the Father, Son, and Holy Spirit created all other life.

The next two phrases of the paternal proper preface name this magnanimity of our vibrant and lustrous God. God did not hoard his goodness but allowed the light and life to overflow into the creation of humanity, which God graciously created in the divine image. This is the most unassailable truth of every human being. If congregants find themselves weary or in a season of self-loathing, they are reminded that no matter in what state they entered worship, they bear the very image of God. The fundamental value of their humanity can *never* be lost. We need that reminder because in all human beings that image of God we bear is clouded by sin. In the final line, this preface assures those gathered that God did not leave his image bearers in their sin but secured their redemption into new life. It is God who "called us to new life in Jesus Christ our Lord."

That new life is possible because of the resurrection of Jesus, who takes center stage in the prayer "Of God the Son," another prayer available to begin the Eucharist in this season. The prayer proclaims that each Sunday is celebratory because Jesus overcame death and the grave on the first day of the week. Congregants are reminded of why they gather on this day and not another. Every Sunday, even in the ordinary season, is a commemorative celebration of the day Jesus rose from the dead, the day the women came to the tomb and did not find his body (Matthew 28:1-7; Mark 16:5-6; Luke 24:1-10; John 20:1-2, 11-18). For those who live in cultures shaped by Christianity, it may be easy to forget, but it remains true: Jesus' resurrection reoriented time, so what feels normal and ordinary is actually the *new* normal created by his defeat of death.

For example, one of my most frequently used apps is the one connected to my local gym. The calendar feature gives primacy to Monday so that Saturday and Sunday fall at the end of each week's row. This makes sense for an organization focused on performance, whose plans begin afresh each Monday; but they do so because Sunday is, even in this culture, typically honored as a day of rest. The disjunct my brain experiences when I look at this calendar makes me realize that the "ordinary" mode of calendars in my culture has a Christocentric shape, where Sunday is typically set as the first day of the week.

We honor this day, even those who do not realize it, because, as the prayer says, Christ overcame two things: "death and the grave." The most extraordinary event in history, the very defeat of death itself, takes place in the midst of the most common human experience, mortality of his body. Either term, death or the grave, would be sufficient to capture the overarching point of what Christ's death achieves, but by including both, the words of the preface evoke his grueling experience on the cross as well as his descent to the dead. He went through the full gamut of the human experience, the moment of death as well as the process of burial, both of which are deeply painful for the loved ones of the person who has died. God willingly experienced these realities on behalf of humanity in the person of the Son. That means that God the Father and God the Spirit experienced the Son's submission to these forces. We are at the edge of the capacity of human language here, but though we are unable to explain it fully, we can say that God, the God of life, *allowed himself* to experience death.

At the same time, those who are gathered in prayer do so because death and the grave were overcome by his glorious resurrection. Jesus is now gloriously alive! This is not only good news for God, but good news for all of creation. He opened to all the way of everlasting life. The congregation can personalize that good news. The way of everlasting life—never again to be interrupted by the crushing grief of death and the grave—is opened to *us*.

It is not just the future to which we look forward, but because of the work of the triune God, we can live into that life of the resurrected Son now. The prayer "Of God the Holy Spirit" captures this reality: "For by water and the Holy Spirit you have made us a new people in Jesus Christ our Lord, to show forth your glory in all the world." It first evokes the themes of baptism. It is by water and the Holy Spirit that a change has occurred. As Jesus promised, the Advocate, the promise of the Father, comes to all those who confess him as Lord (John 14:15-17; Acts 1:5). That spiritual gift is manifest in a tangible way, through water. Christianity always involves the body in the work of the Spirit, and that begins at the very beginning: at baptism. In that work of the Spirit, we become "new people" in Jesus Christ. That means that we are not just waiting for the arrival of eternal life at our own death or at the Lord's return, but we live as new creations now. That may come to light in a plenitude of ways, but all of them will show forth God's glory. The way we live will magnify the truth and goodness of God. This becomes an excellent test for individuals and communities. When we hear this prayer, we are prompted to ask, "Are our actions as Christians bringing glory to God?" If they are only bringing glory to ourselves, or if they are making God seem inglorious, then those are not ways of living blessed by the Holy Spirit. Finally, this prayer reminds worshipers that God did not choose to take us out of the world when we became new creations in Christ but has chosen to leave us in it. We are to "show forth God's glory" in "all the world." That means we are called to display God's glory among our neighbors, in our communities, and beyond. When we do, we draw others to participate in these prayers of praise to the triune God.

It is not only the prayers that invite us to stand in awe of and even participate in God's divine life; so, too, do the Scriptures appointed for Ordinary Time. One might imagine those Trinity-focused Scriptures would arise from the New Testament, texts written once the Son has been revealed in the flesh and the Spirit has been sent to the Church. This is certainly the case, but in the chapters that follow, I demonstrate how truths about the eternal triune life appear throughout the canon, even from the beginning. These texts from Genesis offer many riches for the church to receive as it grows into God's triune life during this season and forevermore. But before the Word, I turn to the sacrament, to discover the other way God chooses to encourage the growth of the church.

4

Feast

If you have the Lord's Supper every week, it won't mean anything." I both thought this and said it out loud to my former youth pastor. He had moved from our Baptist church, which celebrated the Lord's Supper quarterly, to a church in a denomination that celebrated it weekly. When I visited his new church, I sat quietly in wonder at something new but also—I can't deny—with some sense of judgment. As the plates of small bread and small cups were passed along the aisles at the close of the service, it seemed perfunctory to me. In my eyes it seemed to be a rushed obligation to get through before the congregation could mingle and get on to lunch. At that point, I couldn't imagine ever joining a church that did this.

I laugh at (and wish I could scold!) my immature self now. I was being ignorant. It was my church who was doing the historically *unusual* thing of celebrating the

Lord's Supper only a handful of times a year. I was also guilty of hubris, assuming that I "knew" the thoughts and intentions of the people in that room, when their quiet and regular act carried more depth and meaning than my untrained eyes could observe.

At this point in my life, I have now celebrated the Eucharist weekly (and at times more than once a week) for over twelve years, and, rest assured, it has not gotten boring. This is, in fact, the very least I could say. Not only has it *not* become rote, but often those moments are when the Lord does the most profound work in my soul—through the time-tested prayers, through the songs we sing, through the bread and the wine itself.

In this chapter, I invite reflection on this oft repeated and therefore quite ordinary celebration of the meal Jesus commanded us to remember and practice. I begin with reflection on a day the church has set aside to celebrate this meal: *Corpus Christi* (in Latin), "the body of Christ." Then, the bulk of the chapter recounts my own journey from an infrequent participant to (at least) a weekly one, particularly through my perspective as a priest. My aim for readers of this chapter, for all congregants, is an increased awe for this meal. I am deeply convinced that it is one of God's most profound means of grace for the health and growth of the church.

Corpus Christi

The setting aside of a day in Ordinary Time to honor this most regular and therefore "ordinary" expression of Christian worship began in the mid-1200s. It was decided that the church would celebrate the Lord's institution of a meal, given that Maundy Thursday did not lend itself to tones of celebration. The first Thursday after Trinity Sunday was set as the day of this feast. The connection between this Thursday and the Thursday of Passion Week calls the mind back more than a month to Easter and invites reflection on what God has accomplished in the interim through regular acts of grace, including the provision of his own body and blood.

I understand that this meal is complicated. Interpretations of the Eucharist have proven divisive among Christians, from the ongoing pain of prohibiting fellowship at our common Lord's Table all the way to periods of time in which believers employed violence to defend or enforce their interpretive positions. Although during the Reformation many groups ceased to celebrate this day,

Corpus Christi has now returned as a day to honor among many sacramentally-minded Christians. Across the world Christians have reconstituted it as a day to express thanksgiving for Jesus' gift of himself in such a tangible way. To be clear, one need not wade into the complex territory of metaphysical debate to appreciate this day and the supper it honors.[1] This Thursday can be an invitation to contemplate in a preparatory way—on a very ordinary day of the week—what is so powerful about the act we participate in each and every Sunday.

The prayers for this feast day help Christians to see the ways the Lord's Meal touches on the past, the present, and the future. Thomas Aquinas composed some of the early prayers for this day in praise of Christ's body, and they demonstrate the connection of this meal with past promises of God.

> How sweet, O Lord, is your Spirit;
> For you have shown your sweetness to
> your children:
> You have given them most wondrous Bread
> from heaven:
> You fill the hungry with good things and the
> rich you have sent away empty.[2]

The words of this prayer recall the manna God sent from heaven to sustain the people in the wilderness after they had been redeemed from slavery in Egypt. Jesus revealed that this gift pointed to him (John 6:32-35). Aquinas also chose to invoke Mary's words of the Magnificat, which are in line with Hannah's song from 1 Samuel (1 Samuel 2:4-5). Both songs praise the God who will bless abundantly those who humble themselves to approach his table.

Lutheran denominations borrow another of Aquinas's prayers for this day to remember what God will do in those who partake of this meal in the present. The prayer asks, "that we may ever perceive within ourselves the fruit of your redemption."[3] To take these elements into our bodies is like planting seeds in our souls that will result in the fruit of the Spirit in our lives. A perceptive man in my Sunday school class recently observed that some traditions speak about "asking Jesus into your heart," while ours proclaims, "This is the body of Christ," over a piece of bread that we then take into our mouths. All Christians have found ways to follow Jesus' message that God's Word should be internalized (e.g., Mark 7). All Christians aim to receive the promise of the New Covenant that God will plant the good law of God in our hearts and minds

(Jeremiah 31:33; Hebrews 8:10). The Eucharist is a tangible way to enact this internalization.

Finally, the prayers for Corpus Christi recall Jesus' promise that another banquet will take place in the future. They describe the Lord's Supper as "a pledge of future glory . . . given to us."[4] What we practice together now prepares us for the feast of the future, giving us hope that we will celebrate with Jesus face to face.

Prayers for this day remember God's goodness, instill it within us, and await the banquet when no barriers stand in the way between us and God or between each other. Reflecting on this gift intentionally one day each year allows us to notice its innumerable benefits week by week. On the day of Corpus Christi, we pause to remember and prepare for the gift.

Setting the Table

Miller Chapel on the campus of Princeton Seminary was the first place I participated in a Eucharist service in the role of giving the elements in addition to receiving them. A longtime friend who had attended the same college and was now a year ahead of me in seminary invited me to serve as a chalice bearer when he took his turn as chapel preacher, as every senior student had the opportunity to do. Some of my concerns about repetitiveness lingered, but now from the distributive side. I wondered if saying "This is the blood of Christ" to every person who came through my line would get boring. I was shocked and joyfully surprised that the very opposite was true. I found myself praying for every person to whom I handed the cup, with the result that each gift felt as distinct and new as the beautiful individuality of the person before me.

When my family and I first started worshiping at an Episcopal church several years after my first experience of distribution, I found the structure of the service very confusing. They seemed to have a "meet and greet" in the middle, whereas I was accustomed to that time for conversation taking place at the beginning and the end of the service. My husband, who had just finished a PhD in liturgical studies, explained that this arrangement had ancient roots. Everyone could hear the Word, but only the baptized could receive the sacrament, so the "meet and greet," known as "the Peace," allowed space for a comfortable exit. Most churches would not ask anyone to leave at this point, but the break clearly signifies that something different is about to happen.

The service of the Eucharist begins with a series of phrases exchanged between the priest and the people. Named the *Sursum Corda,* Latin for the call to "lift up our hearts," it appears in many denominations' worship services. I am most impressed with priests who can sing these words in the haunting tunes of chant, but even when simply spoken, they always grab my attention. We are acknowledging our presence before the God of the universe as we all express our great gratitude for our salvation.

I have discussed the Proper Prefaces for Ordinary Time in the previous chapter, as three different ways to enact the "right, good, and joyful thing" of giving thanks to God the Father Almighty through the Son in the Spirit. Following the preface for the day comes the hymn Isaiah heard the angels sing, the *Sanctus,* the thrice-repeated cry of God's holiness. Congregants also recall the triumphal entry of Jesus into Jerusalem before his passion as each week they join in the "Hosanna." They are rightly blessing the One who comes in the name of the Lord, the crucified and risen Messiah. There is another one coming in the name of the Lord at that moment too: the priest who ushers the people into this moment of worship. At this point, I either enjoy extending hands of blessing and prayers for a fellow priest or mark the points of the cross on my own body, nearly bowed down in gratitude for the profound grace of standing in this place. Because Jesus is the "he" who comes in the name of the Lord, any and all who are called to the grace of ordination get to participate in this work of Christ and represent him.

In the Book of Common Prayer 1979, five different prayers are available for use at this point in the service. Rite I, from the 1789 BCP, illuminates the desperate human need for God and the answer provided by Christ's work on the cross. It does so in hauntingly beautiful and arresting archaic language. Rite II Prayer A begins with God's infinite love in creation and redemption, with echoes of the *imago Dei* confirmed and healed in the incarnation. By learning from other godly ministers, I have found my body posture enacting the movements of Jesus described. I cannot but help for my arms to extend when I speak of him stretching out his arms on the cross, or draw my arms close to my own belly when I mention him sharing our human nature as a reference to God's decision to send forth his Son, born of a woman (Galatians 4:4).

Prayer B is a bit more expansive, walking through the successive revelation in creation, then in the covenant that includes the gift of the law and the prophets, and finally culminating in the Word made flesh. The prayer calls forth the eloquent opening of the sermon to the Hebrews, proclaiming that we are living in the last days, inaugurated by the coming of Jesus the Messiah, and then names what is assumed by the word *incarnation,* that the Son of God became incarnate from the Virgin Mary. He is the Savior and Redeemer, not just of the few of us gathered on that morning but of the whole world. Because of God's choice to come, to die, and to rise again to eternal life, we are brought "out of error into truth, out of sin into righteousness, out of death into life." My voice rises, my back straightens, and I look the members of my congregation directly in the eye. This is one of the most beautiful summations of the very best news any of us will ever hear. Though my voice often cracks due to the lump in my throat I am seeking to suppress, I have never failed to get through these words, and they have never failed to heal and empower me each time I have the joy of proclaiming them. This is my favorite prayer.

The third, Prayer C, is more expansive still, drawing attention beyond earth, "our island home," to the vast universe God created and over which the Son reigns. Prayer

D, rooted in the Eastern Orthodox Liturgy of Saint Basil, is a rich pastiche of scriptural phrases, from Jesus' first message in the Nazareth synagogue (Luke 4:16-20) to his final prayer to the Father before his capture (John 17).

All the prayers include Jesus' words of institution remembered by the evangelists as well as Paul (Matthew 26:26-29; Mark 14:22-25; Luke 22:19-20; 1 Corinthians 11:23-26), where he took the bread and wine that they were accustomed to sharing and transformed this meal so that it became for them *his* body and blood. It is a rather amazing thing that words uttered thousands of years ago are still repeated all over the world and have been repeated every day for millennia. No matter what divisions taint this table, all Christians recall that it is Jesus who got this practice started. If we do it to remember him, we are being faithful.

At the conclusion of those prayers, the whole congregation joins the priest in the act of spoken prayer. This bodily involvement of the vocal cords revives the minds of any that might have been tempted to wander. In some form or another, the whole congregation declares the past, present, and future work of Christ. He has died. He is no longer dead but fully resurrected, and he will return again, this time not to deal with sin but to bring the fullness of the salvation for which we all wait (Hebrews 9:28).

The next act is done only by a priest. As one who has been ordained, set apart and changed by God, one who stands in the line of the apostles, this person then asks that God would graciously send the Holy Spirit on these simple elements of bread and wine. The priest requests that the Spirit would transform them from something common to something extraordinary, conduits of the grace of God as the body and blood of the Son. Never do I feel more unworthy than at this moment. *Who am I,* I wonder—imperfect, always partially ignorant, with a list of sins I might bring in each week—*who am I to be the material vessel of this miraculous work?* I am no one, and that is the point. The Holy Spirit does not choose the worthy but the willing. As much as is humanly possible, I prepare myself each week to be in a good and right place to be available for this work. The prayer gives me another opportunity to do so. The priest gives voice to what the whole congregation asks, that the Holy Spirit might not just fall on the elements but also on us, setting us aright so that we might rightly receive this gracious gift.

The prayer concludes with a series of prepositional phrases concerning Jesus, saying out loud that he is the center of the entire event. He makes the entire service, the entire world as we know it, possible, and as we join with him, we are caught up into the ongoing heavenly worship of God. This worship gives us hope that our life with God will someday be as clear on earth as it is now in heaven. The connection is even more intimate. We are not just with him, but by the powerful gift of the Holy Spirit we are also *in* him. We participate in Christ in the unification given to us by the Spirit so that we can do what we were created to do, return glory to God, almighty Father, now and forever more.

In a moment of such exuberant praise, one voice is no longer sufficient, and so the whole church joins to say together the prayer that Jesus taught his disciples. As a chorus, we hallow God. We ask that God's will take place here and now as it does in God's heavenly kingdom. What a practical prayer this is. Whatever concern we brought in that day, we can give it to God, asking that the perfect will of God take place. When we pray for this, our eyes are better trained to see that perfect will, even when it does not line up with what we want. Then, we pray for both physical and spiritual provision, being honest about one of our most basic needs, the need to survive, which is the foundation of so many of our more complex needs. If God provides our daily bread, physical or spiritual sustenance, won't God also provide everything else? We also name our need for forgiveness and freedom from the prison of vengeance. Then we ask for protection from ourselves and our chief enemy. These are not expressions of wishful thinking; we pray to the One and only One who has the power and goodness to answer them.

After the Lord's Prayer, the priest breaks the bread. The act of fraction always feels a little violent to me. In my church we purchase "priest's hosts," which are thin, unleavened, perfectly round slices of "bread" (although really, they are more like a very thin cracker). They are about the size of an adult's outstretched hand, perforated into twenty-four pieces. When it is my turn to celebrate and I hold that lovely, perfectly formed circle in the air, and then in the silence break it in two, multiple thoughts and images almost always run through my mind: the rending of Christ's body, broken for us; the abuse he experienced; the rending of the ligaments in his hands and feet; and the breaking open of his side. The breaking of the host evokes what he allowed to happen to him to demonstrate the horrific power of sin. What he allowed to happen destroyed that which causes all destruction. The shattering of the wafer recalls this defeat of death through death.

For several years, I have also thought about the brokenness of the body of Christ in a different sense—the brokenness of his people, corporately. It is a profound grief that not all believers can gather around the same table. When I participated in an ecumenical symposium on the Lord's Supper, we enjoyed meeting one another and learned from the papers given, but the tone at the end was one of sadness, that we could not fix the problem of disunity but only pray for its resolution.[5] While cooperation and friendship are possible in many venues, we are left with the grief that fellowship at the table is split into pieces, just like the host.

Division is not only denominational; sometimes, it is within the local church itself. Week by week, we might find ourselves standing at the altar serving or being served by a person with whom we have profound disagreements or almost unbearable tension. As the bread is split, I often recall the promise in the Twenty-Third Psalm, that the

Lord would set a table for us in the presence of our enemies. I think of Jesus giving the bread to Judas, even though he knew what had happened and would happen. The Lord reminded me time and time again that no matter how broken things were, no matter how minute the broken pieces became that could never be mended by human hands, he could and would put everything back together again. There would be a time when the brokenness would be mended, the confusion cleared, justice done, and relationships restored. The breaking of the bread gave place to acknowledge the pain of division. The promise of eschatological restoration and the brief taste of it around the table should not lead to current quietism. It should instead promote the hard work of honesty and working toward either restoration or healthy separation (think of Acts 15:37-39, where Paul and Barnabas split over their disagreement about John Mark for a time so that they both could continue to flourish in ministry). Just as I've concluded that not all denominations can gather around the table together in the present (while we all see through a glass dimly) but can productively and joyfully work together in other ways, so too with individual Christians we might not all need to be in a working relationship together and, when we are not, there might be more space for some form of healthy relationship.

After the bread is broken in the silence, there is a proclamation of God's grace. Rite I recounts John the Baptist's words that Jesus is the Lamb of God who takes away the sins of the world. Then, it invites the whole church to play the role of the Gentile woman who recognizes her own unworthiness before God. She also knows that God is so abundant that even the crumbs of this table would be more than enough (Matthew 15:21-28; Mark 7:24-30). Then, our church often sings, "This is the feast of the victory of our God," a paradoxical statement at this point that the One who allowed himself to be broken is also the One who won. The priest, one last time, reminds the congregants that these elements are gifts from God. The One who died for us all has invited us to partake of his very body and blood.

The Feast Is Ready

Another of my discomforts on passing from Baptist to Episcopalian was the lack of a weekly altar call, when members of the congregation were invited to express faith in Christ for the first time. The most frequently used hymn for this part of the service was "Just As I Am," whose lyrics allowed the members of the gathering to be honest about their need for God and thankful that God's grace would welcome them with open arms, no matter how they came. I recently attended a prominent, historic Black church in Chicago where this practice occurred in all its beauty and depth. The hymns of invitation played softly through the sanctuary as the pastor gave space and also gave appropriate pressure for congregants to face the gravity of the moment. The call to faith assumes that the church has visitors who need to hear the good news for the first time and be given the chance to say yes to God before they leave and the seed is crowded out by the lusts of the world. It also acknowledges that some in attendance may have heard the message a thousand times but have never been moved by the Holy Spirit until that day. The altar call gives everyone a chance to respond as needed.

I've come to realize that my liturgical church has not abandoned this practice but manifests it in a different form. Each week every member is called to kneel and pray at the altar when they receive the body and blood of Christ, or, if one chooses, receive a blessing instead of the elements. No one is forced to come; you may stay in your seat when your row is called, although the social pressure of most everyone going up is a significant propellant to move. For those who might not be able to overcome the fear of public attention when responding to the altar call as one of the few, the invitation to the Communion rail might allow them to be carried along by the movement of the crowd. When you arrive at the altar and put your body into the posture of humility before God, in many churches, including my own parish, you kneel before a cross. This is a conducive space, time, and bodily enactment to do business with God, to surrender one's life for the first time or the thousandth time. This placement invites congregants to realize aspects of sin that are as yet unsurrendered. This is also a space, time, and bodily enactment conducive for healing, to fall at the feet of Jesus begging for mercy or restoration, as so many do throughout the Gospels. Moreover, the rail can also be a place to express gratitude, to return to God as did the Samaritan leper and express deep thankfulness for what God has done (Luke 17:11-19). The reasons for coming at that moment and what God can accomplish in that moment are endless. When people approach and kneel at the altar, some eyes are bowed in prayer, but some meet mine with intensity.

They express a hunger that I know only God can meet. Often their eyes are moist with tears, indicating that some inner softening is in process. I have learned that, in joining a liturgical church, I have in no way abandoned what was a meaningful and effective aspect of my revivalist-tradition background. Each of us can come "just as I am."

I speak of liturgical worship, of course, with the zeal of a convert. It would not be difficult to find someone who had practiced weekly Eucharist for a good portion of their lives for whom the practice was rote, and therefore meaningless. Such a fact, I would state again to my former immature self, should never be imagined and projected, but could only be confirmed through honest conversation. The potential for such a sad possibility is a good caution to liturgical churches to be on guard against it. It may not be possible to completely avoid it, but the threat of thoughtlessness can at least be alleviated through solid catechesis of what is happening in the Eucharist, with children as well as new members. This could take the form of occasional instructed Eucharist services for those who have worshiped this way for a long time. It is also beneficial to print reminders of the profound truths associated with the Eucharist in the weekly bulletin so that anyone can read and understand as the service is taking place. When appropriate to the text of the week, which is almost always true, the preacher can make connections between the Word and the sacrament in the sermon.

One thing I have stood in awe of in my own former rector is his practice of committing to memory the name of every person in our church (and often their extended family members and their pets!). As they approach the altar, he greets them by name. As Jesus often got the attention of the people around him through direct address, I see this as a powerful way to awaken the person to the work God is doing in that moment. Our church has recently reinstituted a prayer ministry in which congregants can approach a trained prayer minister after receiving the Eucharist to share with another believer more specific needs for prayer, including the desire for conversion. Although church leadership should respect the gravity of this moment of approaching God and duly prepare for what God might do through it, since it is a practice commanded by Jesus it is ultimately the Holy Spirit who will ensure that whatever transformation needs to happen through it, will. Leadership can steward this work, but we cannot control it. It is sobering to remember that we cannot manipulate the spiritual encounter in the meal. It is comforting to recall that if the practice is enacted according to Jesus' command, even if it is done imperfectly, no human can completely thwart the action of God in this gracious gift.

The act of sharing food is a familial one. The person before me, no matter their age or their social status, humbles themselves through the bodily act of kneeling; if kneeling is not possible, then the humbling of themselves can happen through the act of requesting the bread. They do not take it; instead, I hand it to them. Repeatedly, this act strikes me as very parental. This is amplified if they elect for me to give them the cup as well. It reminds me of the years in which my husband and I helped each of our children learn to drink from a cup, or when my mother-in-law was in the last season of her life and the family helped her to do the same. She struggled with the cup not, of course, for lack of experience, but because of a lack of control over the body, that loss that comes with age and infirmity. Hence, the priest or lay minister who distributes the elements is serving others as a parent would serve a child or a child would serve an ailing parent. Each person who comes for the Eucharist is willing to express a neediness, a lack of control, that puts us into the framework of a child, exactly the posture Jesus said would be necessary to enter the kingdom (Mark 10:13-15).

When everyone who desires to do so has been fed, it is the job of the servants for the day to clean the table. I almost always recall Kathleen Norris's story that when she attended a liturgical service for the first time, what made a great impact on her was the fact that the priest "did the dishes."[6] As the corporal cloth laid out to catch the crumbs of the broken bread is folded at the end of the meal, I think of the disciples who handled the cloths that surrounded Jesus' body, either the linens with which Mary swaddled him (Luke 2:7) or the grave clothes that Nicodemus and Joseph of Arimathea used to wrap the crucified body of Jesus (Matthew 27:59; Mark 15:46; Luke 23:50-53; John 19:38-40). These are such common and even messy parts of human experience, and our most holy experience with God recalls them every time we eat this bread and drink this cup. By returning the table to its barren and common mode, we prepare the space for the holy encounter all over again.

For a number of years, I alternated leadership of the Eucharist at a weekly gathering of faculty and staff at the college where I teach. The minister who invited me to participate hailed from the Reformed tradition. The service he provided for our gathering closed with this prayer: "With burning hearts we thank you, Father, for making Christ known to us in the breaking of bread and in the poured-out wine."[7] The body of Christ now exalted at the right hand of the Father is mysteriously and graciously present in the elements consecrated and distributed, and having taken Christ inside of us, we all depart as living members of the body of Christ asking for strength and courage to love and serve God. The God of the universe has invited us to dinner and made himself the meal; there is nothing ordinary about that. If we did it only once, that would be amazing, but the grace of God is so abundant that he will meet us in this way as often as we approach. God has ensured the growth of the church through the gift of this meal. Ordinary Time is the perfect season to reflect on this extraordinary gift.

5

Image of God

Near the end of Ordinary Time, the church prays a collect that calls on God, "who caused all holy Scriptures to be written for our learning" (Proper 28). This prayer's focus on God's Word distills the Anglican doctrine of Scripture. Composed for the 1549 Book of Common Prayer, it has endured as a vital reminder for a people of the Book. God is to be blessed because the Lord of all did not remain silent but communicated with creation through creation. Also, God communicated with words. Because of our finitude, immaturity, and entanglement internally and externally with sin, through our own faults and through what has been done to us, we are often unable to hear these words of God with perfect clarity. We do so always through the static of our human position. Hence, we must ask that the God who graciously gave these words will also "grant us so to hear them, read, mark, learn, and inwardly digest them." Only then can we achieve the end for which God gave them—namely, that "we may embrace and ever hold fast the blessed hope of everlasting life" given in our Savior Jesus Christ. This penultimate prayer of Ordinary Time propels us to consider the gracious benefits of the Scriptures that are appointed for this season of growth and throughout the church year.

The Revised Common Lectionary provides two tracks for the Scriptures read in the worship service each Sunday during Ordinary Time. In one system, the Old Testament passage is chosen to align with the theme present in the Gospel reading. In the alternative option, the readings move chronologically through the Old Testament: one year focuses on the Pentateuch, one on the history and Wisdom literature, and one on the Prophets. In this path, at the end of three years, congregants have gained a decent sense of the scope of the first testament's story.

I have chosen to focus on several of the readings from this chronological track, ones that come from near the beginning of the Bible. These are stories that concern the family with whom God first established the covenant. They appear in the first year of the lectionary cycle, near the beginning of Ordinary Time. I have chosen to give attention to them not only because starting at the very beginning is, generally, a very good place to start, but also, more substantively, because these stories provide a template for the ways in which God breaks into our experience of the ordinary and transforms it. God meets Abraham, Sarah, Hagar, Ishmael, and Isaac in the mundane events of life with some unparalleled divine interventions. Similarly, God meets all of us, both subtly and shockingly, and asks for our faith. When we trust in God, even in the smallest ways, we grow and are then ready to trust when God meets us in the big things. The life of this family demonstrates that growth in faith, a vital demonstration we all need to hear in this season of growth.

The next three chapters of the book trace this growth of trust in the various members of this family. I first focus on the image of God revealed in the story of Genesis 18. In order to trust God, we must first see God and see the way that God values each of us. Next, from Genesis 21, I highlight the ways Sarah and Abraham, as well as Hagar and Ishmael, continue to grow (or need to grow) in trust. Finally, in the heart-wrenching Genesis 22, I focus on the lesson Abraham teaches the church, not as an example we are meant to replicate but as a signpost for which we are meant to be thankful. Hearing these stories in this season helps us see God, trust God, and be thankful to God. Ultimately, they teach us to have faith in God. Journeying along with their story in Ordinary Time aids our own growth.

Abraham Sees God

Readers meet Abraham in Genesis 12, which includes the account of God's initial call to him and his family (at that point, he is "Abram"). His father, Terah, had already determined to move their family from Abram's birthplace, Ur of the Chaldeans, to go to the land of Canaan. They had traveled about six hundred miles to Haran when Abram's father died. At that point, it would have made good sense for Abram to go back to the land of his birth. He surely had more connections there than in a new land or in Canaan, a land to which he had never been. Surprisingly, it is at this juncture that Abram responds to God's call—"Go to the land that I will show you" (Genesis 12:1). In his response, Abram demonstrates a brave faith. The narrative does not disclose any previous relationship with God nor indicate any family traditions with God on which he could rely. He is the beginning of the covenant history. It must be the case that, even without much history, he was so in awe of the presence of God that he responded and obeyed.[1]

In addition to God's promise of a land, God promised Abraham descendants. "I will make you a great nation," God says (Genesis 12:2). There is a challenge, however. Earlier in chapter eleven when Abram's wife, Sarai, is introduced, the first thing said about her is that she is barren. It also mentions that Abram is seventy-five years old. Admittedly, people lived longer in Genesis than they do today, but nevertheless, the odds are stacked against them to receive this promise that begins with a child.[2]

The promise of descendants and the difficulties of obtaining that promise form a consistent thread throughout the story of this family. A few chapters later when God reiterates this promise,[3] Abram pushes back a bit, saying in effect, "What will you give me God, since I am childless? How is that you will give me a land and make me to be a blessing to others if I have no heirs?" (Genesis 15:2-3). God again promises that he will have a child from his own body, and Genesis tells us that again Abram believes God.[4]

When Sarai does not conceive, in collusion with the culture in which she is caught, she provides her slave, Hagar, and Abram *does* have a child from his body through her. Hagar bears Abram's first son, Ishmael. This occurs when Abram is eighty-six years old (Genesis 16:16).

As recorded in the next chapter, when God proclaims the covenant to Abraham yet again (and, in Genesis 17:5, changes his name), God promises explicitly that Abraham will have a child *through his wife,* whose name God changes to Sarah (Genesis 17:15-16). Abraham laughs. At this point thirteen years have passed since the original promise, and still Sarah has had no child. We might recount his exasperated statement to God thus: "I'm about to be one hundred, my wife ninety. I already have Ishmael. Why don't you let him be the child of the covenant?" God promises to bless Ishmael but reiterates that the covenant will be through Sarah's son, a son yet to be born (Genesis 17:19-21). Then, to enact the covenant between him and God, Abraham follows some demanding divine instructions (Genesis 17:10-14): Abraham, Ishmael, and all the men of his household are circumcised (Genesis 17:23-27).

This is the event that precedes chapter eighteen. As the curtain opens on this scene, Abraham is sitting at the entrance of his tent in the heat of the day. On the one hand, this could be a rather ordinary scene. In the heat of the day, at the normal time of the afternoon rest, Abraham is sitting at the entrance of his tent. On the other hand, his life at this moment is anything but ordinary. For twenty-five years God has promised Abraham a child, and now God has asked Abraham to be circumcised, to cut the part of his body used to produce a child. Hence, as he is sitting there in the heat of the day, maybe this is not a normal rest. Maybe he sits in desperation, maybe in pain—he whose life has been turned to anything *but* normal by his faith in and obedience to God. He is sitting and waiting. What else can he do? It is at this moment, when the promise seems most unlikely, that God shows up.

The first verse discloses to the reader the real nature of this encounter: it is the Lord who is making an appearance to Abraham. Readers will recall that in Exodus when Moses asked to see God's glory, God said no, and stated that if anyone saw God's face, they would die (Exodus 33:18-20). God's glory would simply overwhelm a sinful human being. In this instance with Abraham, then, God appears in a form that does not destroy the one who sees. God mediates the holy presence so that the interaction *can* occur. It is a double act of grace. First, God deigns to interact with a person when God could just leave the person alone. Even more, God does so in such a way that the humans are preserved in the midst of a divine encounter.

The reader knows all of this, but Abraham does not. When he looks up, all he knows is that three men are standing before him. Upon seeing them, immediately he springs into action. He runs to them, tells them his plan for their visit—probably speaking it as he's coming up with it!—and then enlists members of his household to make it happen. In addition to preparing a lavish meal, he stands ready to serve the needs of his guests while they eat it. I might prefer my hosts to sit and eat with me, but Abraham's attention does show his fastidiousness for their care.[5]

Because the reader knows what Abraham does not, many of his actions serve to excite the reader, because he's doing *all the right things* to greet God. He bows before his visitors, enacting the posture of worship. He addresses the three men with a singular title, my Lord. He positions himself as their servant. He prepares a lavish meal for them of the best flour, the best meat, the same things that will be instructed for the sacrifices in the tabernacle (Exodus 29; Leviticus 2). Moreover, he does so in massive quantities for such a small group. By treating these guests with the most excellent respect, he has entertained God unaware.

A famous icon renders this scene visually. Created by Russian iconographer Andrei Rublev in the 1400s, this has been hailed as the greatest achievement in Russian religious art. Many Christians have seen it as a fitting icon for the season of Ordinary Time. This is when we live in contemplation of the good life we can grow into because of the life that flows to us from the communion of self-giving love at the fount of all life—namely, the persons of the triune God. The three visitors in the icon share a unity. They are all the same size; they each have the same length staff; they each sit on a throne; they are each clothed in blue in some way. They each look toward one another, creating a circle of visual movement among them. On the other hand, they are distinct, three persons with differences in dress and positioning. Our finite minds can never grasp the beautiful truth that our God is triune, but this visual depiction invites us not to fully understand but to contemplate the beauty of three in one.[6]

Readers also learn something from Abraham's actions, actions we can emulate. When we recognize and respond to the humanity of those we encounter—strangers as well as friends—we are respecting the image of God in them. Abraham's overwhelming hospitality prompts us to ask in this season, "Who in our lives do we need to love without reserve? Who do we need to be willing to be interrupted by?" We might, as Hebrews instructs, meet a stranger who is actually an angel (Hebrews 13:2), but even if that surprising event does not occur, we can rest assured that every person we meet bears the image of God and should be treated as such. Jesus too instructs his followers to treat others as we would treat him (Matthew 25:34-46).

In some ways, seeing the good in a stranger might actually be easier than seeing the good in someone we know well, in friends, family, and even in ourselves. To learn that lesson, let's consider Sarah.

God Sees Sarah

Once the elaborate meal is done, the divine visitors get to the business of the visit. They speak with one voice: "Where is Sarah your wife?" (Genesis 18:9). Their question is the first indication that they have interest in her directly, not only interest in what she can provide for their refreshment. I wonder if her ears perked up when she heard her name. She had not been introduced to these guests. How did they know who she was? This might be the first indication to Abraham and Sarah that these visitors are not normal humans.

Saying her name is especially interesting because she had just undergone a name change. In chapter seventeen, God said to Abram that his name would change to Abraham and that his wife's name would change from Sarai to Sarah. Both are forms of the same name, which has royal connotations. If you had been called one thing your whole life, and then because of God's directive began to be called by a different derivation of that name, it would be noticeable. We call our daughter Katherine by the nickname Kate, but if all of the sudden we had a vision from the Lord to begin calling her Kathy, that would be striking. In Sarah's case, the name change was necessary because it was attached to God's promise *to her*. In chapter seventeen, God told Abraham that the promise for descendants would come through her. *She* would bear the child of the promise. The narrative does not say if Abraham passed this information on to her or not. But when she hears her name from these three guests in a form unusual to her, surely, she begins to pay attention. Then one of them speaks about a future visit when something very unusual—in fact, something seemingly impossible—will happen. By the time of that return visit, she will have a son. If Abraham hadn't told her about the exchange he had with God, when God twice said that she would be the mother of the covenant, she is now hearing it from the very mouth of the Lord!

The narrator pauses at this point to remind the reader of what has been said about Sarah multiple times. She is not a winning candidate for having a child. Recall the first thing said about her is that she is barren. Multiple times readers learn that she is old, and here for the first time the text says that she is post-menopausal. As is true for Abraham, so too for Sarah. If this couple is going to have a baby, it will be a miracle. Nothing natural in their bodies will make this likely. It's laughable really, and so, she laughs. With a giggle, she refers to herself not just as old but as "worn out" (Genesis 18:12). How could someone past her prime, who was barren during her prime, ever experience the abundance, the joy, the pleasure of having a child? When the Lord next speaks to Abraham, the question reveals that God knows exactly what is going on, not only in the tent but even in the inner monologue of Sarah. The Lord asks, "Why did Sarah laugh? Is anything too miraculous for the Lord?" (Genesis 18:13-14).[7]

Sarah was totally within bounds to laugh. It was beyond reason to think that she and Abraham would have a child. Nevertheless, she then denies her very understandable laughter out of fear. What a normal response when God sees us completely, when God speaks truth about us. We, like Sarah, are tempted to deny what God has exposed. God responds simply with the facts: "Yes, you did laugh" (Genesis 18:15). It is striking that in this moment God and Sarah are having a conversation, a back and forth, and yet the story never says that Sarah leaves the tent. Hence, this conversation happens even through the barrier of the tent. This is a powerful picture of the truth that no barrier blocks God. In effect the Lord's conversation with Sarah communicates to her, "I hear you. I know you, your disbelief and your denial, and even in light of that, I will still choose to bless you."

God's choice to bless Sarah is a bit unsettling. Both before and after this event she treats Hagar horribly. It does us no good to gloss over those hard truths, to try to deny them like Sarah denied her laughter. She's married to a slave owner and treats Hagar as a slave. She's caught in the matrix of a sin common to her time, and she willingly participates in it. She uses Hagar's body and then becomes jealous of the birth she orchestrates.

Shockingly, at the same time, she is a princess in God's kingdom. Sarah truly gets to live out her name. It is not just through Abraham (who himself is a mix of good and sinfully frustrating actions) but also through *her* that the covenant comes. She is the mother of the covenant, a distant great-grandmother (we can add many more "greats" to this) of Jesus himself. To state it bluntly, Sarah does not deserve the good she gets. If I were choosing, I'd choose someone more worthy.

This story about God miraculously and undeservedly blessing Sarah really drives home the point of Romans 5:8, the epistle reading for the same Sunday in Ordinary Time: "While we were still sinners, Christ died for us." As a theological data point this sounds beautiful, and I can give my full assent. But when it becomes personalized, it gets real, and therefore I feel my resistance to it rise. Sinners like *Sarah*? I need to think about that a bit more to see if I approve. The more I study Old Testament exemplars of the faith, the less I like them, the more I see their warts, and the more I wonder why God chose them.

But who could God choose? There are no perfect people. Everyone has some ugliness because everyone is caught in and culpable for sin. No one is deserving of what God gives. But instead of leaving us in our mess, God comes to save us and to bless us. God begins the line of redemption instead of leaving humanity on our own, and God begins it even through people like Sarah. God is willing to show grace to her, and that teaches us that God is willing to show grace to everyone. The *imago Dei,* the image of God, in every single human, no matter how limited they might be, no matter how dastardly, is the perpetual reminder of God's ever-present and unconditional grace. When we face the truth that we do not deserve God's blessing and yet God gives it anyway, we can more easily celebrate and cultivate God's image deposited in all those around us, those strangers I don't know and the friends I know too well, who also unassailably bear the image of God. This generative tale in the life of Abraham and Sarah, preserved in text and art, when three visitors possibly gave a glimpse of the invisible, triune God, might train our eyes to see all those around us and ourselves as made in the same beautiful image.

In Christian experience, instead of preparing a meal for God, God prepares a meal for us and invites us to come to his table, where he gives the most lavish feast of all: his own body and his own blood. When we come to this table, we can see ourselves as clearly as God sees us, as honestly as God saw Sarah—sinful yet blessed, always bearing God's image. As we grow in this understanding about our triune God and ourselves made in God's image, with God's grace we will be prepared to graciously give that same grace to whomever we encounter and invite them to the same lavish table, to commune with the God whose image they bear.

Genesis 18 gives us some vital insights for how we might contemplate our triune God, see and serve God's image in others, and accept the indestructible image of God in ourselves. These are not just interesting theological insights; they can change the very way we live. When we see God and accept that God sees us, we've taken the first step toward growth in trusting God. We've taken the first step in growing in our faith, living faithfully in the Ordinary Season, the season of growth.

6

Trust

The triune God is the God of life, and therefore the God of growth. If the call of the church during Ordinary Time is to grow in faith, then that begins with seeing God and acknowledging that God sees you. The growth of faith is then followed by trusting God. The lectionary's next story of Abraham, Sarah, Hagar, Ishmael, and Isaac read during this season of the year provides examples of the benefits of trusting God. Although some of the events of their lives are part of ordinary (and often heartbreaking) human brokenness, others are unparalleled moments of God's intervention. Congregants who hear these passages in worship can learn trust from both. In order to experience the growth of this season, we must learn to trust the One who causes all growth, even and especially through the most difficult of experiences. To trust God is to trust that God is working all things for our ultimate good. This is one of the most ordinary lessons of faith, that the story of each member of this family teaches in a slightly different way.

Celebration Interrupted

Given his seemingly impossible existence, it makes very good sense that Isaac is cause for a party. The party takes place when Abraham and Sarah have had their miracle baby, and, even more, when Isaac has lived through the very precarious time of early life (Genesis 21:8). When children were weaned, typically around three years of age, ancient parents breathed a little easier because it would finally seem likely that the child was going to make it.[1] The promise appeared secure for Isaac, so it was time to celebrate.

The next event follows so directly that it seems that it takes place at the same time, suggesting that something goes wrong right in the middle of the party. Let's consider this event and what unfolds from it from the perspectives of each person in the narrative.

Sarah and Abraham

In the midst of this celebration, Sarah notices her son with his older half brother Ishmael. She sees a teen playing with a three-year-old, and Ishmael is laughing. That does not seem like a problem inherently. After all, this is the same action Abraham and Sarah engaged in when God told them they would have Isaac: they laughed (Genesis 17:17; 18:12). That laughter is the cause of Isaac's moniker; his name means the child of laughter (Genesis 21:6). Sometimes the word does have negative connotations of being unkind, but it could also be the case that when Sarah saw Ishmael doing the thing that was associated with Isaac, she felt protective for the uniqueness of her son. The possibility that she felt threatened by Ishmael finds confirmation in the next sentence. She did not want Ishmael to inherit with Isaac. She has good reason. In the ancient world women would be dependent on the inheritance given to their children.[2] Ishmael was Abraham's first-born son, so typically he would get more and, because she did not have a good relationship with his mother (see Genesis 16:6), maybe Sarah worried that Ishmael would cut her son and her out of their share. On the other hand, several times over God had promised inheritance to both of Abraham's sons and had never wavered in the promise that Isaac was the child through whom the abundant covenant blessings would proceed. Sarah knew in her body that God can take nothing and bring life out of it. God had demonstrated miraculous abundance in Isaac's birth. She should have known that no limit limits God, that with God's provision there will always be more than enough. Nevertheless, she worries about Ishmael's competition with her son. It is evidence that she has forgotten God's abundance. It is frustrating that Sarah could not trust God's provision for both her son and Ishmael, but it is also understandable. We, too, often fail to trust that God will provide, even though God has provided abundantly—even miraculously—in the past. As much as we might not like to admit it, we are not unlike Sarah.

Maybe Abraham's focus had been elsewhere during the party, enjoying the congratulations of his neighbors, but in Genesis 21:10, Sarah grabs his attention with a startling request: "Drive them out." The verb she chooses communicates the intensity. Interestingly, this is only the third time in the Bible thus far that this verb has been used. The other two instances include God driving out Adam and Eve after their initial disobedience in the garden, and then God driving away Cain after he killed his brother (Genesis 3:24; 4:14).

When Sarah comes to Abraham and says the same words, "Drive them out!" Abraham might well have wondered, *Who?* Sarah, leaving no room for any misunderstanding, provides the answer right away: "This slave woman and her son." In her speech, Hagar and Ishmael are not even given the dignity of their names. Despite her poor motivations, curiously, God instructs Abraham to do whatever Sarah says. On the one hand, it seems unjust that God would go along with an action motivated by fear and selfishness. On the other hand, since Sarah was failing to trust God's provision and since she had already kicked Hagar out once (Genesis 16), then it could be the case that God was showing mercy. By allowing Sarah to kick them out, God was freeing Hagar and Ishmael from their slavery, so they wouldn't have to be around Sarah any longer and could receive their blessings from God out from under her paranoid gaze.

In Abraham's eyes, though, this thing Sarah demanded was very distressing. In fact, this is the only time in the entire Bible that this word for distress is paired with the adverb "very." The language indicates that Abraham *hates* this suggestion.

Recall that when God told Abraham that Sarah would have a child, Abraham asked for God's attention not to leave Ishmael (Genesis 17:18). Abraham continually showed concern for him. That doesn't mean that Abraham does not also care for Isaac. His love for them is not a zero-sum game, but mutually reinforcing. For if he treated Ishmael with contempt, could Isaac trust that someday Abraham might not do the same to him? He loves both of his boys. God assures Abraham, as God had stated previously, that blessing would still come to both of his sons: both would become fathers of nations (Genesis 21:12-13).

The next day, the day after the party that had *not* ended joyfully, Abraham rose early. He took provisions, simple ones of bread and water. This was not enough for Hagar and Ishmael to relocate, maybe because he trusted that God would provide whatever else they needed. But giving them these simple things allowed Abraham to demonstrate a tangible expression of his care. The passage even says that he helps put the backpack of water on Hagar's shoulder. What a tender detail. Even though it was painful for him, Abraham obeyed God: he sent away Hagar, the mother of his child, and his own first-born son. On this morning, Abraham had to give Hagar and Ishmael to the care of God. Abraham needed to begin to practice giving up what he loved when God asked.

Hagar

Abraham is being as caring as he can while being faithful to the God who is freeing Hagar and her son from Sarah. It is unlikely, however, that Hagar experienced this release as a redemption, at least not initially. The story is not clear at what point Hagar learned of her fate. Was it that evening at the party? Did she overhear Sarah's demand to Abraham? Or was it early that morning when Abraham woke her and presented her with bread and a skin of water, unusual gifts if it was a usual day. When Abraham tells her that he is going to send them out, he uses a different word than Sarah's "cast out!" It is softer and not so intense. For Hagar, however, that's just semantics; the action is the same. She is cast out of her home and community with her teenage son. She is consigned to wander, and the word for wandering conveys not a sense of exploration, but a sense of aimlessness. With just a little bread and water, they are consigned to walk around until they run out of resources. They are aimlessly walking as they wait to die. Then, they do run out of water, and the countdown to their final moments begins.

Reading this account elicits a visceral response in me to the point that I find it difficult to read. I had the privilege of being able to nurse my children. I know what a gift this is, but commensurate with this grace also came hyper vigilance about their thirst. Something in my body and mind changed, and I became and remain to this day ever anxious that my children have enough to drink. For Hagar to run out of water to give her son seems to me the cruelest of desperate situations.

When they run out of water in a way that likely I never will, she casts her son under a bush. This is the same term used when Joseph's brothers throw him into the pit, an action to get rid of a body that will soon be dead. She is at the end of all hope. She goes a distance away because, as she says, she doesn't want to see her own child die (Genesis 21:16). It is striking that she is thinking of her boy at this moment. If there is no water, she is in as desperate a situation as her son, but she thinks of his death above her own.

Maybe she gets just far enough away from him so that she can cry without him hearing her, because it is not until this point that she lifts up her voice and weeps. I imagine that Hagar cried so hard it felt like her insides were being emptied out.

The beginning of verse 17 is incredibly powerful: God heard. These are the cries of a displaced slave woman rising from the middle of the wilderness. She was in a place where no one could hear her, and she was a person few people would care to listen to. But God did. God heard. God heard her cries for her son and listened to her and to him. It is here we learn that Ishmael must have been crying too, and, of course, he was the primary reason for her cries. God attended to the object of her tears, the aim of her lament. As she wanted, God paid attention to her cries by paying attention to her son.[3]

God then interrupted their tears. The angel of the Lord speaks to her from heaven *by name*: "Hagar." This one word speaks loudly. It demonstrates that God knows her name and will speak it, a choice quite opposite from Sarah when she made her demand of removal to Abraham. The question God speaks, however, at first seems a little odd. The Hebrew could be translated, "What's up with you?" I can imagine her exasperated response: "Oh, you know, my child and I are about to die. And how are you?!" What seems like an insensitive question exposes the reality that even death itself does not warrant hopelessness when God is involved. God is about to reveal to her that things are not as desperate as the conditions around her indicate. Alternatively, the Hebrew could also indicate God's care.

A fitting translation of the question is also, "Hagar, what do you need?" God hears in her cries the fear that lies underneath: the fear of death, the fear of failing at the most basic responsibility of a parent—namely, to preserve the life of one's child. The angel assures her that God has heard the voice of the boy where he is. God knows her son better than she does and cares for his life even more deeply than she does. For a parent aching for a child, this is a deep and abiding assurance.

Instead of giving up and distancing herself from his pain, God calls her to take him in her arms. Then God speaks to her the promise he has already communicated to Abraham: "I will make of him a great nation" (Genesis 21:18). If Ishmael has a divinely promised future, that means he will make it through the deathly present.

Then God opened Hagar's eyes to see a well. It was there all the time, but in her despair she had not noticed it. At times, we too realize the answers are close to us when the haze of fear and despair dissipates. She filled the water vessel and gave Ishmael a drink. It is difficult to imagine what a joyous relief that must have been for her. Once they had been restored, they kept wandering until they found a place and people. They could do so, of course, because God was present with them. God directed them to a particular place and people, and that was to the people of Egypt.

This is the end of Hagar's story.[4] When she is introduced in Genesis 16, she is referred to as an *Egyptian* slave girl. That means that at the end of her story, Hagar was among her own people. Having been redeemed from her slavery, having spent time in the wilderness, where she cried out to God and God met her need, she now gets to go back to the people of her land. You can hear, I'm sure, how her story previews what happens to the descendants of Isaac: redemption from slavery, wandering, divine provision, and return. Her story is a vital signpost to what God will do with and for Israel.

Ishmael

We must also consider the story from the perspective of Hagar's son, Ishmael. I wonder how he interpreted Isaac's birth. He's an early teen, and although culture has changed, then, as now, this is a liminal, in-between age. This time when humans are in the process of finding out who they are feels awfully precarious because "who you are" is yet untested. During this time in Ishmael's life, the miraculous birth of Isaac occurs. If the order had been reversed, if Isaac had come first, Ishmael wouldn't have existed at all. Surely, he realizes that. At this party for the long-hoped-for son, it could very well be that Ishmael was laughing at Isaac in a mean way. Readers are not meant to condone that action, but it is understandable. At that vulnerable age, and in those degrading circumstances, he laughs. Given that context, even this kind of "laughing" does not seem to justify the punishment he receives, to be expelled from the only home he's ever known.[5]

Although this decision centered on him, likely he was the last one to know about it. Sarah told Abraham, Abraham told Hagar, and last of all, probably very early on the morning of their departure, Hagar woke Ishmael to tell him of their fate. The wandering wouldn't have been exciting for him. They had nowhere to go and not enough provisions to get there. Likely by the time she cast him under the bush, he was exhausted and weak with hunger and thirst. Maybe he didn't let himself cry until she was some distance away, and she couldn't hear him over her own weeping. But God did. The child of slavery. The child of contention. The child who had always seemed like a mistake and was now not necessary at all. The child who posed a threat. Disposable and now disposed. And God heard *him* cry. God restored his mother from her despair, so she could fittingly care for him.

This was not a one-time intervention. God remained with Ishmael until he fully became a man. The place where he was cast off became his training ground. Had he not lived in the wilderness, he would not have become skilled with a bow. In chapter 16, the angel of the Lord had promised Hagar that Ishmael would be wild and contrarian. This doesn't necessarily mean "bad." It could also indicate that Ishmael was free and critical of the world system as it was (Genesis 16:12). Interpreted this way, this promise became true. Ishmael did not live under slavery anymore. He lived in the wilderness; he lived free. Moreover, by virtue of his growing up, he had plenty of reason to critique the world system into which he was born. He became a man who could see clearly because God had seen and heard him. God was with him, Genesis says (Genesis 21:20). Eventually he married and had a family of his own. God had promised him an inheritance, and God kept that promise, even when it seemed impossible.

God

There is one more character in this story—God. I took a class in graduate school on the narratives of the Old Testament and our gentle and godly professor, Dennis Olsen, taught us to ask this question: "Where is God in the story?"[6] This is not to bring God down, to make him one more actor among the others; rather, it is to recognize God's grace, that God has deigned not to stay distant from our stories but to enter into them.

God is present and active from the very beginning of this account, in the lives of each member of this family. Isaac exists and grows healthily by the provision of God. That does not suggest, however, that God sent Isaac so that he could take what was Ishmael's and replace him. God had a plan and a purpose for both of them. God had promised enough for both, nations from each boy. It reminds me of another story, told by Jesus, when the older son begrudges the celebration for the younger, but the father reminds him that everything he needed had always been available to him (Luke 15:11-32). As mentioned, God did not condone Sarah's motivation for her action against her slave woman but used it for the good of Hagar and Ishmael, to free them from slavery and provide for them directly. Since God is the source of all compassion, it is God who stirred Abraham's heart to feel distressed, and to provide bread and water so that they could wander for a while until they discovered the provision from God.

It is when Hagar and Ishmael are most desperate that God's presence and action are most visible. When Hagar places Ishmael under a bush and says, "Do not let me look on the death of the child," to whom is she speaking? Maybe she is just vocalizing what is in her head, but when we do so and we think we are alone, of course, God is listening. Alternatively, as a woman of faith (as evident in chap. 16), with this statement she could be calling out to the God who hears. Fittingly, God does so. God hears her, and God hears her son. It seems that God had been directing their steps—what felt aimless to them was actually providence. They ran out of water just as they approached a well. After that, God stayed with them, gave them a place to hunt, gave them a family, and bequeathed to Ishmael a grand inheritance. It is important to note that Ishmael received his inheritance not through Abraham and the system of rape and slavery in which they were all caught, but directly from God.

In relationship with this providing God, they each learn to trust. Sarah needed to learn to trust that God can provide for her *and others* without competition. Abraham had to learn to trust God by giving up what was dear to him to God's care. Hagar learns to trust that God cares for her child even more deeply than she does. Ishmael learns to trust God that he was not a mistake and that God would use even his hardships to make him a skilled and insightful man. They didn't learn four different lessons, but four different facets of the same lesson. They all learned to trust God because God is trustworthy. God is intimately involved with this messy family, giving them freedom to make choices, but working those choices, even the bad ones, for their ultimate good.

The question for worshipers who hear this story during Ordinary Time, unsurprisingly, is this: Where do *you* need to trust God? Where do you need to give something up, to trust that what God has given you is enough, even if it seems like someone else has more? Where do you need to trust that God can love those you love even better than you can, that you need not be a savior to them but direct them to *the* Savior? Where do you need to trust that you matter to God and that God has a good plan for your life? The record of this moment in the life of this family can facilitate our own trust in God, in all the ways necessary to maintain what is for the people of God not extraordinary, but ordinary radically trusting faith, week by week, day by day, during celebrations and those that get painfully interrupted.

7

Gratitude

The stories of this family read from Genesis during Ordinary Time instruct the church to grow by seeing God and trusting God. The final account that I will discuss, the story of Abraham and Isaac from Genesis 22, invites another basic practice: gratitude.

The Tree

Once, when I was going through a hard time in my life, a friend showed up on my doorstop with a tiny sprig in a large planter. "I didn't know what to do," she apologized, "so I brought you a tree." She and her husband farm, so this was a perfect expression of her creativity and care.[1] That little tree still sits on my front porch, not big enough yet to plant. Trees serve as signs of endurance for generations beyond, signs of a life beyond the present moment. They are signs of hope, signs that make us grateful.

An arboreal reminder of grace features prominently in this next story of Abraham's life. However, a little bit of background is necessary to understand this story fully—specifically, a reminder of the identity of a man named Abimelech. He's the king of Gerar, a region where Abraham was traveling in Genesis 20. This is one of the two regions where Abraham passed off Sarah, his wife, as his sister. Because God protects Sarah when Abraham doesn't, Abimelech and his people encounter the power of God. This leaves Abimelech both in awe of Abraham's God and quite cautious of Abraham. When he approaches Abraham in Genesis 21 and says to him, "God is with you in all you do" (Genesis 21:22), that's a pretty loaded statement. The tone of that statement suggests the sentiment: "I don't want to end up on the wrong side of your God again, so I'm going to tread lightly around you." To make things clear, he adds, "Please don't deal falsely with me."

I wonder how Abraham felt at those words, "God is with you in all you do." Maybe it felt ironic to him at that moment. He might have thought, *I've just had to send my oldest son into the wilderness. I'm not exactly feeling the warmth of divine favor presently.*

Readers learn that Abimelech has approached Abraham because their people have gotten into a disagreement about a well. After several negotiations that involve the exchange of gifts, they agree that the well belongs to Abraham. That might not seem like a big deal to us, but if my guide in Israel said it once, she said it a hundred times: "This is a thirsty land." Kingdoms rise and fall based on their access to water, so control of a well is no small thing. Abraham plants a tree near this well and calls on the Lord as *El Olam,* "the eternal One." Remember that Abraham is a sojourner and an alien in this land, but to secure a well and to plant a tree indicate permanence. These are signs of putting down roots. Moreover, when he does these acts, he calls on God as the eternal God. Maybe he's made peace with what happened with Ishmael, or at least it's not as prominent in his mind after some time has passed. He has a son, Isaac; he has a well. He is feeling settled. Maybe he imagines that things will never change.

This is when, the narrator reveals, God tests him.

The Test

I've not met too many people who like tests. Even if someone enjoys school, tests bring a certain amount of anxiety. One of my husband's most beloved professors in college called exams "opportunities." She did it with a wink and a smile, knowing it would elicit groans and eyerolls, but I also think she believed that is what tests were, opportunities. Tests were opportunities both to demonstrate what students had learned and to continue to learn more, even through the process of taking the test itself.

Similarly, readers would be correct to say that God is giving Abraham an opportunity to demonstrate what he's learned.[2] If a test takes place after one has learned the material, then Abraham had learned what it meant to give up a son he loved, to trust him into the care of God. And now he's going to be tested on the same concept.

We might wonder—and God is big enough to receive our questions—if it is morally right for God to test someone. Shouldn't God already know what is going to happen? Why put Abraham through the pain of it all? This honest question gives us an insight into God's gracious nature. God is eternal and knows all things, but because Abraham is human, a being within time who does not know all things, a test allows him to discover for himself, experientially, what it is to obey

God. He can receive the joy of success through this test. God tests humanity so that we might learn that we are capable of doing the right thing and grow in our ability to avoid sin. This test of Abraham is seen as the summit of his lifelong (and admittedly imperfect) walk with God. Here, by the gracious act of testing, God allows him to learn the depth and effectiveness of his trust in God.

At this time in his life, when things seem settled, when he's planted a tree and secured a well, God puts him to the test. To initiate the test, God calls out to him, "Abraham." And Abraham responds, "Here I am" (Genesis 22:1).

Abraham was used to hearing from God. This is the eighth recorded time that God invites Abraham into a conversation. Abraham was used to listening and had learned how to respond. Even more, he had learned how to respond *immediately*. Even with this knowledge, I doubt Abraham had any idea what God would say this time.

It could be the case that God's command begins gently. A Hebrew term that can be translated as "please" is attached to the command for "take." Its presence shapes the tone in which we hear God talking. A gentle statement reminds us that God knows what Isaac means to Abraham, knows better than Abraham himself.

The conversation that follows is communicated in language that is meant to be read slowly, spaced out with consideration for each phrase.

"Please take your son, your only one" (Genesis 22:2).

I imagine Abraham winced at that. It is God's acknowledgment of his pain and obedience in that he's already given over the only other son he had.

"Take the son whom you love and go to Moriah" (Genesis 22:2).

Abraham might have thought, *So we are going on a trip? That's wonderful!*

"And offer him there" (Genesis 22:2).

At this point, I can imagine Abraham thinking, *Sure, I can do some sort of ritual by which I commit him to you, Lord. Like a baby dedication, or better, because he's older, like a confirmation. That will be a meaningful moment, and then we'll come back home.*

"Offer him as a burnt offering. Wholly consumed" (Genesis 22:2).

God is saying, "You will not bring him home. You will not even hand him over to me as you did with Ishmael. It will be your hand directly that commits his life to me. You will not send him off; you will watch him die." This is a shocking and totalizing request.

Sometimes Abraham talks back to God, asks questions, or makes counteroffers. Not this time. He is silent. Verse 3 tells us that he rose early in the morning—just as he had with Ishmael when he sent him and Hagar out. It is the same phrase exactly. Surely, like the reader does, he was remembering that morning with Ishmael on this morning with Isaac.

As part of his preparations, he cuts wood. It isn't clear if he cuts down the tree he's just planted. It is simply stated that he takes some tree, a thing that conveys settledness and rootedness, and he removes it by chopping it down. It will create the fire that will consume his child's body once it is slain. Nothing seems settled and rooted to Abraham now.

It takes three days of walking before they arrive at the place God appointed. Consider a time when you had something hard in your future, something difficult that you knew was coming. The time between your present and that hard thing seemed to stretch out indefinitely. I imagine Abraham was quiet during those three days. The others might have been chatting or joking, telling stories and singing songs as people often do on a long walk, but not him. He held the truth of the trip within him.

Even in his verbal silence, he must have been conversing with God in words that are not recorded. This is evident because God had only said, "Go to the mountain I will show you"[3] without disclosing the particular mountain. By the third day, God had let him know on which mountain in the area this would happen.

When he knows the place and that it is time for him and Isaac to depart for it, Abraham tells the servants who were traveling with them, "*We* will come back." Interpreters have wondered if he is lying so as not to raise their concern. If they knew he was going to kill Isaac, they surely would have intervened. Alternatively, possibly he is disclosing to them what he's not said to God, that he's really not going to go through with it. This seems unlikely for someone who has had so many conversations with God; certainly, he's aware that he can't lie to God. Another option is that this statement is evidence of his faith. That is how the epistle to the Hebrews interprets him. Hebrews 11:19 says, "He considered the fact that God is able even to raise someone from the dead." Abraham could have deduced that if it was God's will that this boy be the bearer of the covenant promises, then he would have to stay alive and continue the family line. In other words, Abraham would have believed that no matter what he did, if he was obeying God, God would give his son life. Hence, he can say in trust, "We, not I, will come back to you." That he trusted God seems to be the best interpretive option.

As he and his son depart from the group, he asks Isaac to carry the wood he's cut, that tree he removed. Abraham laid wood on him, knowing that he's about to lay him upon the wood. As Isaac carries the wood, Abraham carries the fire starter and the knife; he carries the instruments of death.

Genesis reveals that, at this point, the two of them walked on together. The emotion in Abraham in this moment is impossible to capture in prose. He loved this miracle boy. His hopes rested on what God would do through him. Even if he trusted that God could raise the dead, the act of slaying him by his own hand, of bringing fear and death to the one he loved—there are no words to describe the weight he must have been carrying.

But this is not known to Isaac. At least, not immediately. "Worship" for him would mean sacrifice of some sort. As they walk, Isaac does the cultic math and comes up short. Fire, check. Wood, check, but no lamb. After making this observation, he asks his dad about this absence. "God will provide the lamb" (Genesis 22:8), Abraham replies. Abraham doesn't scare Isaac with this answer. He doesn't say more than is necessary, but also, Abraham doesn't lie. It is an answer of wisdom and trust. It indicates that Abraham still has faith in God's provision. It seems that he's doing well on this test. That answer suffices for Isaac. For the second time Genesis says, "The two of them walk on together" (Genesis 22:8).

In verse 9, Abraham builds an altar for the sacrifice, takes that tree he's cut down, the wood he's chopped, and arranges it. Even after all this, still, no other lamb has shown up. At some point in the midst of verse 9, although the words are not recorded, Abraham communicates to Isaac the full truth of this trip. The silence here is deafening. What is *not* described speaks volumes. In the moments between the arrangement of the wood and the binding of Isaac, Abraham has revealed the truth and Isaac doesn't disagree. Isaac doesn't run away. He doesn't fight.

Earlier the narrative states that much time has passed since the party to celebrate Isaac's weaning (Genesis 21:34).

This suggests that Isaac isn't three years old anymore. Commentators imagine him anywhere from his teens to middle age. Certainly, he is old enough to choose to submit himself to this process. Old enough to stand still while Abraham binds him, picks him up, and lays him on the wood. The two of them are no longer walking together, but they are *working* together. They display their individual and mutual trust in the God who can raise the dead. It is evident that Abraham has passed on this resurrection faith to his son.

Abraham goes all the way to the point of taking the knife, the knife with which he would soon kill his son, and preparing it for the slaughter.

But then, "Abraham! Abraham!"

Isn't it good that Abraham had learned to listen and respond immediately to God's call? As he said at the beginning of the chapter, he says again: "Here I am." He's still listening, still ready to hear and obey, and willing to stop what he's in the act of doing and hear what God would like for him to do instead. God says out loud what Abraham already trusts is true about God—that God desires absolutely no harm to come to Isaac, that nothing should hurt him (Genesis 22:12). Abraham has passed the test.

Then, at this moment, the story draws attention to the ram. Just like Hagar with the well, the answer was there, but the eyes of the person being tested had to trust God first before they could see the provision. Father and son offered up this animal, the one provided by the Lord, in an act of profound gratitude and worship. Abraham gave the mountain a name that meant, "the Lord provided."

In response, God reiterates the covenant blessing already given to Abraham multiple times by this point (Genesis 22:17-18). In this iteration, God adds a poetic description to the promise of the descendants from Isaac. They will not just be as numerous as the stars, as stated previously, but they will also be as plentiful as the sand on the shore. The promise is now, literally, grounded.

At the end of the account, Abraham goes back to the well he'd built previously, that place where he began putting down roots. But there is one fewer tree there when he returns. That tree he used for the sacrifice is missing. There is a space where once stood the tree he used for the whole burnt offering that, indeed, God had provided. With the absence of that tree and the presence of Isaac, I imagine Abraham feels more grounded than ever before. The first grain of sand is in his hand—his son

Isaac is at home. Consequently, Abraham trusts in a way he has never trusted before. He trusts that that lone grain, because it has, in a metaphorical way, fallen in the ground and died, has now been returned to him. Through its "death" that grain will multiply into a number he could never fathom.

The Lesson

This is a chilling account. We might wonder what kind of God instructs his follower to sacrifice his child. Maybe no physical harm comes to Isaac, but what about the psychological damage inflicted on him? If your dad bound you and raised a knife over you because God said so, that would be a dastardly form of religious trauma. This assessment of a capricious God might be appropriate if this account was lifted out from all the others. But seeing it embedded in the whole of Abraham's story, the whole of Genesis, the entirety of the Scriptures of Israel and the New Testament, this assessment of evil in God is not fitting.

I am convinced that Genesis teaches that Abraham went through with this because, by this point, Abraham knew who God really was. Abraham knew that death was no barrier for God. His and his wife's reproductive systems were as good as dead, and yet, here Isaac was. He knew that God was so sovereign and so abundant that God could provide for and bless the son he sent out into the wilderness. Abraham trusted that even the emotional strain of getting to this point, because God had commanded it, would be for his *and Isaac's* ultimate good. Abraham's faith was not blind; it was based on many miraculous interventions in his life before this moment.

God did not give this test to Abraham until God knew he was ready to pass it. And he did. The voice of the Lord through the angelic messenger says, "Now I know that you fear God." God could say to Abraham, "I have experienced with you as you experienced it in real time the evidence that you trust me fully. You've shown me, you've shown your son, and you've shown yourself your wholehearted devotion, not in theory or promise but in (willing but uncompleted) action."

This story in the Bible is different from many others. It does not ask us to put ourselves in Abraham's or Isaac's shoes, to wonder what God might be asking us to give up. There are other passages that teach that lesson without the frame of child sacrifice (Matthew 19:27-30; Luke 18:22;

Philippians 3:8). What Abraham and Isaac were willing to do serves as a signpost, not as a template. The fitting response here is not repetition, even of the metaphorical kind, but simply gratitude.

Christian readers have always seen how this event points the way to Jesus. It previews his willing walking and working with his Father, who is the God who is able to raise the dead. With the death of Jesus the Son, by the power of the Holy Spirit, God proved that identity. By encountering this story of Abraham's and Isaac's willingness, readers are compelled to give thanks for what our God was willing to do fully: experience death in the person of the Son in order to defeat death once and for all. We know we aren't God or Jesus, but neither are we Abraham or Isaac, the first patriarchs of the first covenant. God will never ask anyone to replicate the signpost because this story has been fulfilled forever in reality. We don't need to do anything like Abraham and Isaac because their willingness has been fulfilled forever in Christ.

How fitting it is that after reflecting on this event through the Liturgy of the Word, the congregation is invited to celebrate Christ's meal. We remember and participate in what the Lord did for us by willingly giving his own life. Hence, the lesson of this climactic story from Abraham's life is quite simple: say thank you. Express gratitude for the sign and, most of all, express gratitude for the reality. Being grateful for what God has done—previewed in Genesis and accomplished in Christ—is a necessary step toward daily faithfulness. That daily faithfulness is when trust, even in the face of death, becomes our new ordinary.

Conclusion

Christ the King

I have attended my own church on Christ the King Sunday only once, and this was during Covid. The annual meeting of my academic guild takes place over that weekend, so I am always in the city where it is held. If I do not have a session I need to attend, I find my way to a local congregation. While I miss the majesty of this service at my own parish, it has been powerful to see Christ's kingdom extended to many different places.

This closing week of Ordinary Time is not an ancient celebration. Instituted by Pope Pius XI only about one hundred years ago, it was created to remind Christians of the sovereignty of their Lord in the face of seemingly indefatigable forces of evil that were manifesting in many nations at that time. Sadly, the need for such an acknowledgment seems evergreen.

As Ordinary Time begins its final weeks, the attention begins to shift away from the here and now to focus on the future. Given for use at the end of September, the collect for prayer asks that the church be not anxious about earthly things, but "love things heavenly; and even now, while we are placed among things that are passing away, to hold fast to those that shall endure" (Proper 20). The following week proclaims that we will be "partakers of your heavenly treasure" (Proper 21). These prayers do not encourage an escape from the good work to be done in God's good creation. They *do* remind the ones praying that—thankfully—the system of the world as it currently exists will not endure forever. The collect for the culmination of the season said during the service that celebrates Christ as King articulates the hope built on the truth of Jesus' reign. It affirms that it is God's will "to restore all things." Because the Son of God and he alone is "King of kings and Lord of lords," it is only his gracious rule that will redeem and unite those currently "divided and enslaved by sin."

In the first year of readings (Year A), the reading for this day from Ezekiel 34 and Psalm 95 or 100 conveys the gentleness of his leadership, articulating his role as the

Shepherd of the sheep. The letter to the Ephesians read this week proclaims his sovereignty over every "rule and authority and power and dominion, and above every name that is named, not only in this age but also in the age to come" (Ephesians 1:21). Paul's language here is unabashedly comprehensive, in line with so many other New Testament authors who reflect on Jesus' fulfillment of Psalm 110:1. All things, and that really means all things, have been put under his feet.[1] If believers feel comforted by this fact, and they should, the Gospel reading also provokes them to interrogate their own need to submit to Christ's sovereign command. In Matthew 25, Jesus asserts that at his coming, he, as King, will judge each of us, not by our allegiance or aversion to any human power but by our tangible expressions of love for those in need.

The readings from the lectionary in Year B express the hope for the just reign of David's descendant (2 Samuel 23; Psalm 132) or provide the vision of the enthroned One in Daniel 7, Psalm 93, and Revelation 1. Through the Gospel reading congregants hear Jesus answer Pilate, the Roman governor, without pomp but with incredible power: "I am a king. For this I was born, and for this I came into the world" (John 18:37). The third year (Year C) unites the themes of shepherding with the hope for David's son, the just and caring King (Jeremiah 23:1-6). The epistle text from Colossians proclaims his sovereignty, not in a way that he appears distant and uninvolved, but with the truth that his rulership is played out at the most intimate level. All of creation—even our very bodies—holds its coherence because of him (Colossians 1:17). The Gospel reading from Luke features Pilate's ironically truthful sign over Jesus' head as he promises the repentant thief a welcome into this kingdom (Luke 23:33-43).

This day in the church calendar offers the opportunity for the congregation to join in the singing of several triumphant hymns. "Alleluia! Sing to Jesus" begins with an acclamation of Christ's scepter and throne. The next two verses focus on the personal experience of his reign, that he is near us even though we cannot see him and that he is the intercessor and friend of strangers, to whom we can direct our plea. Written by a businessman, W. Chatterton Dix, the hymn does not lose itself in the spirituality of Jesus' kingdom but grounds his sovereignty in common human experience. This is also true with "At the Name of Jesus," a poetic rendition of the Christ hymn in Philippians 2:5-11. This song fills out the lines of the scriptural poem with a full verse for creation, the humiliation and exaltation of Christ, Christian life, and the parousia. The words express the hope that someday "all wreaths of empire [will] meet upon his brow." Until then Christians can rest assured in his reign and claim him as "King of glory now." Written by an Anglican woman, Caroline Noel, who was afflicted with physical illness and loneliness, this poem was penned for those who were experiencing their own darkness and was offered as a reminder that Jesus is in control even when his reign is hidden from our experience.

In America, Christ the King falls in the latter half of November, and every other year, this is just a few weeks after national elections. For as long as I can remember, these have been seasons of incredible anxiety, vitriol, and even deep despair. Although the two sides of the political spectrum agree on almost nothing, they do seem to share a sense that the world is deeply broken and the end of the good life as we have known it is at the doorstep. This is not just an American issue; country after country have morphed as sections have come under the spell of an angry nationalism. Today's world seems in just as much need for the proclamation of Christ as the true King as it did one hundred years ago. Maybe that connection across time sheds light on the possibility that there is never an era without trial, nor is there ever a generation that does not feel beleaguered. Some Christians resisted the setting aside of this special day to proclaim Christ's kingdom because they argued Christians should proclaim his lordship every week, on every day, with every breath. I am of the opinion that to have a day set aside to do so, through prayers, readings, and songs, causes us not to miss the power of that confession. No matter what we groan under, personally or corporately, he has already defeated it. Proclaiming our hope for his kingdom on this last Sunday of Ordinary Time causes us to long for his return to set it up on earth as it is in heaven. That longing leads us perfectly into the season of Advent.

But before moving into that season, it is beneficial to reflect one final time on this one. Writing on Ordinary Time was a daunting task. Not only does it comprise the majority of the church year, but it also includes all the basics of the faith. What we do in this season is the normal, the control, the fundamentals we should do in every season. Selection of topics, then, given their expanse, was necessarily subjective. My prayer is that the themes and texts I have chosen might be illuminative and challenging, encouraging and empowering for those who live year after year through this long and rich liturgical season. Jesus walked through many ordinary days during his life, and during them he grew in wisdom and stature, in favor with God and others (Luke 2:52). Even on the days in which we might have thought that nothing happened, through the eyes of faith we realize that when we cultivate the simple practices of corporate worship, communal prayer, mutual encouragement, and personal reflection, by God's glorious grace, even and especially on those ordinary days, we too experience growth. Now, by the power of the Holy Spirit, he walks with us, revealing his glory to us, clothing us with his honor, providing for us at his table, and inviting us to train in the ways of trust and gratitude. Because we journey with the One who, on the radical days as well as the very many ordinary ones, grew, we the church can do the same.

Acknowledgments

I'm so grateful to Esau McCaulley for including me in this beautiful series and to the whole team at InterVarsity Press for guiding me through the process, especially Ted Olsen. Listening to or reading the other volumes not only taught me much about the church year and Christian worship but also gave me a sense of the series. I'm honored to be included in such an august group of scholar pastors.

I always appreciate my husband's editorial eye, but he, as a PhD in liturgical studies, was especially helpful with this project, both in finding sources and in confirming that I was describing everything correctly.

Because I ventured into writing about the story of Abraham's family, several of my colleagues who are specialists in that part of the canon, Andrew Abernethy, Aubrey Buster, and Michelle Knight, graciously read early drafts and provided necessary insight and correction.

I'm also grateful to Rob Ribbe, Ashley Kiley, and the entire HoneyRock community for first receiving the sermons that became these chapters.

St. Mark's Episcopal Church is the amazing community where I get to do ministry. I'm so grateful to all of them for how they have helped me learn about God's goodness in this season and all the others as well.

I wrote the first draft of this book in one of the most non-ordinary times of my life, the summer of 2023. I'm grateful God counted us worthy to endure that season and provided me wise saints to help me do so: Angela, Genalin, Alli and James, Elizabeth, Deri, Amy, Emily, Andy, Dan, John, Beth, Joyce, Andrea, Esau, and countless others. Whether you read this book in a time that is largely ordinary, especially joyful, or incredibly hard, I can testify of what I know in the depth of my soul: God is with you and is using all things for your good and your growth.

Notes

Introduction: The Ordinary Season

[1] Communicated beautifully in the documentary *Godspeed,* which reflects on the pace of Jesus' walking. *Godspeed: The Pace of Being Known,* directed by Danny Lund (Chalmette, LA: The Ranch Film Studios, 2016).

[2] Tish Harrison Warren, *Liturgy of the Ordinary: Sacred Practices in Everyday Life* (Downers Grove, IL: InterVarsity Press, 2016).

[3] Kayla Craig, *To Light Their Way: A Collection of Prayers and Liturgies for Parents* (Carol Stream, IL: Tyndale Momentum, 2021).

[4] Andrew Peterson, "Forward," in *Every Moment Holy, Vol. 1: New Liturgies for Daily Life,* edited by Douglas K. McKelvey (Nashville, TN: The Rabbit Room, 2017).

[5] The work of Rebecca Larson appears at "The Art of Liturgy," accessed October 18, 2023, www.etsy.com/shop/TheArtofLiturgy.

[6] These prayers are named "proper" in that they are "proper" to that week in the church year.

[7] Philip H. Pfatteicher, "Ordinary [Ordered] Time," in *Journey into the Heart of God: Living the Liturgical Year* (New York: Oxford University Press, 2013), 306–9.

[8] Douglas Kaine McKelvey, *Death, Grief, and Hope,* in the Every Moment Holy series, vol. 2 (Nashville, TN: Rabbit Room Press, 2022), xiii.

[9] It was N. T. Wright who clarified for me the truth that Christianity believes in "life after life after death," in *Simply Christian: Why Christianity Makes Sense* (New York: HarperCollins, 2006), 16. See also Kevin W. Hector, "The End," in *Christianity as a Way of Life: A Systematic Theology* (New Haven, CT: Yale University Press, 2023). Exegetically I see this revealed in Hebrews, whose author holds together Christ's divinity and sinlessness alongside his growth in perfection (Hebrews 2:9; 5:10; 7:28). As Christians participate in

him, we too can anticipate being free from sin and death and also able to grow into the heights of God's call on our eternal lives. Since God's holiness is infinite and we are becoming holy as God is holy, that will be an unending process. Christian perfection is not static but ever deepening.

1. Green

[1] Everett Ferguson, *Baptism in the Early Church: History, Theology, and Liturgy in the First Five Centuries* (Grand Rapids, MI: Eerdmans, 2009), 36, 58, 466.

[2] Ireneaus, *Adversus haereses* 4.20.7.

[3] Esau McCaulley, *Sharing in the Son's Inheritance: Davidic Messianism and Paul's Worldwide Interpretation of the Abrahamic Land Promise in Galatians* (London: T&T Clark, 2019).

[4] See an example of this in Esau McCaulley et al., eds., *The New Testament in Color: A Multiethnic Bible Commentary* (Downers Grove, IL: IVP Academic, 2024).

[5] Biblical instructions are provided for how to live within it when the system cannot be changed. See Esau McCaulley, *Reading While Black: African American Biblical Interpretation as an Exercise in Hope* (Downers Grove, IL: InterVarsity Press, 2020), 139-63.

[6] Gratitude to Emily McGowin for imparting to me this powerful image.

2. Bold

[1] John Meade Falkner, "After Trinity," in *Collected Poems* (Leicestershire, UK: The John Meade Falkner Society, 2005).

3. Triune

[1] Marjorie Reeves and Jenyth Worsley, *Favourite Hymns: 2000 Years of Magnificat* (London: Continuum, 2006), 38-40.

[2] Philip H. Pfatteicher, "Ordinary [Ordered] Time," in *Journey into the Heart of God: Living the Liturgical Year* (New York: Oxford University Press, 2013), 288.

[3] Pfatteicher, *Journey into the Heart of God*, 291.

4. Feast

[1] Although if one wants to, I highly recommend James Arcadi, *An Incarnational Model of the Eucharist* (Cambridge, UK: Cambridge University Press, 2018).

[2] Philip H. Pfatteicher, "Ordinary [Ordered] Time," in *Journey into the Heart of God: Living the Liturgical Year* (New York: Oxford University Press, 2013), 306-309, 294. The citation can be found in Saint Thomas Aquinas, *Opusculum* 57, 1-4, translation from The Divine Office, vol. III (London: Collins/Dwyer/Talbot, 1974), 31-32.

[3] Pfattreicher, *Journey into the Heart of God*, 294.

[4] Pfattreicher, *Journey into the Heart of God*, 295.

[5] I recognize that as a Protestant, my colleagues in the Catholic and Orthodox churches might gently posit that the solution is simple: I could return to the mother church and mend the division. The fact that two different bodies would urge for my return demonstrates that the problem is not only a Protestant one. For the written work that came out of this conference, see George Kalantzis and Marc Cortez, *Come Let Us Eat Together: Sacraments and Christian Unity* (Downers Grove, IL: InterVarsity Press, 2018).

[6] Kathleen Norris, *Quotidian Mysteries: Laundry, Liturgy, and "Women's Work"* (New York: Paulist Press, 1998), 2-3.

[7] "The Lord's Supper (1994)," Christian Reformed Church, accessed June 30, 2025, www.crcna.org/resources/church-resources/liturgical-forms/lords-supper/lords-supper-1994.

5. Image of God

[1] Gratitude to Rev. David Fisher, priest at Trinity Episcopal Wheaton, for this insight.

[2] Because this child is the catalyst through which blessing will come to all people (Genesis 12:3), God's ability to overcome any limitation to ensure the birth of this child reveals the depth of God's desire to bless all humanity.

[3] In the very next scene after God first gives the promise, Abram passes off Sarai as his sister rather than acknowledge that she is his wife; in so doing, he puts her in danger (Genesis 12:11-13). God doesn't give up on Abram after this selfish act.

[4] This is when his belief was accounted to him as righteousness (Genesis 15:6).

[5] Abraham's hospitality is in sharp contrast to the failure of hospitality in Sodom and Gomorrah in Genesis 19.

[6] Gabriel Bunge, *The Rublev Trinity: The Icon of the Trinity by the Monk-Painter Andrei Rublev*, trans. Andrew Louth (Crestwood, New York: St. Vladimir's Seminary Press, 2007). Interpreters have debated if this biblical scene is meant to gesture toward the Trinity. In the next scene, the passage describes

the messengers as two angels (Genesis 19:1). What is clear from this passage is that God has initiated an encounter with Abraham and Sarah.

[7] This truth strikes a beautiful resonance with Gabriel's statement to Mary at the Annunciation, when, in response to her question about the logistics of a miraculous birth, he states that nothing is impossible with God (Luke 1:37).

6. Trust

[1] Claus Westermann, *Genesis 12–36*, trans. John J. Scullion, A Continental Commentary (Minneapolis: Fortress, 1995), 338-39.

[2] V. H. Matthews, "Family Relationships," in *Dictionary of the Old Testament: Pentateuch*, ed. T. Desmond Alexander and David W. Baker (Downers Grove, IL: InterVarsity Press, 2003), 291-99.

[3] This is the meaning of Ishmael's name.

[4] This is the last readers hear of her other than in a genealogy list (Genesis 25:12), where she is named as Ishmael's mother.

[5] The form of this verb indicates a negative connotation, as in "mocking," but there is no indication in the Hebrew text of something really dastardly, as in sexual immorality, although that appears in some midrash of this text. Gordon J. Wenham, *Genesis 16–50* (Dallas: Word Books, 1994), 82.

[6] His work can be found in Dennis T. Olson, *The New Interpreter's Bible Commentary Volume II: Introduction to Narrative Literature, Joshua, Judges, Ruth, 1 & 2 Samuel, 1 & 2 Kings, 1 & 2 Chronicles* (Nashville, TN: Abingdon Press, 2015).

7. Gratitude

[1] Tiffany Eberle Kriner is also a gifted teacher and writer. You can read her story and learn from her wisdom in *In Thought, Word, and Seed: Reckonings from a Midwest Farm* (Grand Rapids, MI: Eerdmans Publishing, 2023).

[2] This is one of two times that God tests an individual in Israel's Scriptures (see also God's test of Hezekiah in 2 Chron 32:31). All the other times, God is testing the whole people of Israel, Abraham's many descendants.

[3] Much like God did when he first called Abraham to go into an unknown land. This, too, is evidence that he is being tested on lessons he's learned in the past.

Conclusion: Christ the King

[1] See Hebrews 2:5-10 for another example of the author's emphasis of this truth.

The Fullness of Time Series

Each volume in the Fullness of Time series invites readers to engage with the riches of the church year, exploring the traditions, prayers, Scriptures, and rituals of the seasons of the church calendar.

Lent
Esau McCaulley

Christmas
Emily Hunter McGowin

Easter
Wesley Hill

Epiphany
Fleming Rutledge

Pentecost
Emilio Alvarez

Ordinary Time
Amy Peeler

Advent
Tish Harrison Warren